DEDICATION

To my oldest Son and dear little buddy, Stephen.

Number 2491 has a long string of coaches in tow as it leaves
Oakland with a Big Game Rooters' Special on November 22,
1947. *Fred Matthews photo from the collection
of James H. Harrison*

PACIFIC

2472's FAMILY ALBUM

Freight Extra 3250 west and train No. 243, pulled by Pacific 2485, leave the huge Sacramento complex at approximately the same time on March 16, 1947.

J.C. Hammond photo from the collection of Walt Grande

PACIFIC

2472's FAMILY ALBUM

KENNETH G. JOHNSEN

INTERURBAN PRESS
GLENDALE, CALIFORNIA

About the Author

DR. KENNETH G. JOHNSEN is a dentist in Kent, Washington. His love for Southern Pacific steam locomotives dates back to his childhood in his native California. He has written several previous books, including another on S.P. steam, *Daylight: 4449's Family Album*. A prolific writer and photographer, Dr. Johnsen's byline has appeared in virtually all of the railroad magazines. His photographs have won awards in both local and international photographic exhibitions.

Ken was married to Lauri Ainsworth in 1972. Son Stephen was born in 1982 and son Gregory was born in 1989. Stephen shares Ken's enthusiasm for trains and photography. In addition to model trains, the Johnsen collection contains a couple twelve-inch-to-the-foot examples. Asarco Number 4 is a 1937 Davenport 0-4-0 which Johnsen leases to the Camp Six logging railroad in Tacoma, Washington. And Northern Pacific caboose Number 1324 is currently undergoing restoration as a guest cottage.

Trolleys also interest Dr. Johnsen, and in 1973 he persuaded the City of Yakima, Washington, to inaugurate trolley service over the existing lines of the Yakima Valley Transportation Company. He has been a motorman there on summer weekends ever since.

Library of Congress Cataloging-in-Publication Data

Johnsen, Kenneth G., 1946–
    Pacific : 2472's family album / by Kenneth G.
      Johnsen.
      p. cm.
    Includes bibliographical references.
    ISBN 0-87046-092-7
    1. Pacific (Locomotive) 2. Southern Pacific Railroad Company. I. Title.
TJ603.3.S6J84   1990
385'.0973—dc20   89-26723
                                CIP

FRONT COVER: The most famous S.P. Pacific, the 2472, crosses the bridge at Palo Alto in an original watercolor by Howard Fogg from the Alan Miller collection.

REAR COVER: A streamlined P-10 (left) races along north of Bakersfield in the summer of 1941. *Steve Peery collection*. P-14 No. 651 (right) gets the *Sunbeam* moving out of Houston in 1953. *Joe R. Thompson photo*

Design and Production
Brueggenjohann/Reese Creative Services
Typography
Roc-Pacific, Los Angeles, CA
Printing and Binding
Walsworth Publishing, Marceline, MO

Table of Contents

Introduction

Class P-3, S.P. Sacramento, 1917 *James E. Boynton collection*

THERE ARE STORY BOOKS and there are picture books. There are encyclopedias and there are poems. Is the last word on a subject ever really written? Probably not.

The book in your hands is a fond look at the 4-6-2 type locomotives of the Southern Pacific as seen through the eyes and lenses of those who worked on them and admired them. Visual appreciation of the esthetic evolution of this locomotive type as well as a pictorial look at its operational history remains the theme of this volume. The roster and appendix provide certain mechanical information, but I will leave it to the Churches and the Kratvilles to record the nuts and bolts details.

A number of knowledgeable steam veterans have given unselfishly of their remembrances and their photograph collections to this effort and I would like to thank two in particular, my friends Jim Boynton and Bob McNeel, for adding real flavor to this book.

Every book on steam locomotives really should take a good look at their tenders too. Extra special thanks go to Arnold S. Menke, the undisputed authority on S.P. tenders, for providing photos and the material for Chapter Three.

Harre Demoro shares my unabashed love for the Pacifics, and his enthusiasm and magnificent photo collection helped keep the fires going on this project from beginning to end.

Others who were only too happy to help included Robert A. Campbell, Sr., Mac Gaddis, Walt Grande, Tom Gray, James H. Harrison, Nils Huxtable, Bob Kern, Stan Kistler, Peter Kunedt, Arthur L. Lloyd, A.D. McLennan, Mike Mangini, Alan Miller, Iris Myers, A.M. Paine, Kenneth Roeh, Joe Strapac, Joe R. Thompson, Harold K. Vollrath, Wilbur C. Whittaker, and Ted Wurm.

Thanks are also due Mac Sebree and Paul Hammond of Interurban Press for bringing this project to its final fruition.

The next chapter in the Pacifics' story is being written today in the efforts of Bay Area volunteers to bring one or more of these handsome machines back to life. May 2472's Family Album provide inspiration and historic perspective to the generations who will fall in love with the Pacifics because of what these volunteers are doing today.

Kenneth G. Johnsen, D.D.S.

Pacific Family Album

PACIFIC. The term conjures visions of our nation's westward expansion to the shores of the vast Pacific Ocean. In the lexicon of railroaders, Pacific is the name given to steam locomotives of the 4-6-2 wheel arrangement (four leading wheels under the smokebox, six driving wheels under the boiler, and two trailing wheels under the firebox). Pacifics were used by a great number of railroads throughout the United States, including the Southern Pacific.

To understand the Pacifics' niche in the history of steam locomotives on the Southern Pacific, it is helpful to look at them as one of the important steps in the evolutionary development of high-speed dual-purpose locomotives.

Nineteenth Century ancestors of the Pacifics were the American (4-4-0) type engines which established the validity of the four-wheel leading truck as an aid to better tracking and more even riding characteristics. Increasing the capacity of the locomotive boiler meant lengthening the frame upon which it rode.

A pair of wheels placed under the firebox yielded the next level of the evolutionary chain: the 4-4-2 Atlantic. Southern Pacific was still ordering new Atlantics when the first Pacifics arrived on the property.

The support of the trailing truck at the cab end of the Atlantics and Pacifics provided a bonus in better riding qualities. Crews involved in the long fast runs peculiar to railroading in the western United States appreciated the smoother ride on these engines. (Pacifics hauling name passenger trains on the Overland Route actually covered more than 500 miles without change.)

Pacifics were used at one time or another on every division from New Orleans to Portland and while the Southern Pacific considered its 4-6-2s dual-purpose locomotives, the class was used principally in passenger service.

They were well remembered for their service on the "Over-Nite" manifest freights and rush merchandise/perishables trains, to be sure. And they could be found in helper service on some districts and on an occasional drag freight (their high drivers showering the tracks with sparks in defiance to the excessive tonnage). Local freight service, when for some reason other engines were not available, was at times entrusted to the Pacifics, too.

The Pacifics' lair, however, was usually associated with the centers of passenger movements and many made their homes at Oakland, Mission Bay, Sacramento, Los Angeles, Fresno, and San Jose roundhouses.

Let's look at numbers. Of the 112 4-6-2 type locomotives on the railroad's Pacific Lines roster, 90 were built specifically for S.P. These included all the 2400s (2400-2491 inclusive) owned by the railroad. (The 2476 and 2477 were built as 701 and 702 of the Arizona Eastern. In 1924 S.P. consolidated some of its subsidiary companies into the parent system. Arizona Eastern was one of these and with it came the two Pacifics.)

The 2400s were joined by 20 locomotives numbered in the 3100-series (3100-3109 and 3120-3129) in 1924. These engines were part of the roster of the El Paso & Southwestern which the S.P. absorbed in that year.

Southern Pacific's Texas & New Orleans subsidiary was served by 37 Pacifics in the 600-series (600-633 inclusive and 650, 651, and 652). The first 22 engines arrived on the T&NO numbered in the 900-series. They were soon renumbered into the 600s and all subsequent arrivals continued in that order.

The 650, 651, and 652 were streamlined rebuilds of the Pacific Lines' 2455, 2456, and 2457. Thus, the total number of Pacific-type locomotives rostered on the entire S.P. system was 146 locomotives.

Some 4-6-2s of the Pacific Lines found employment for a time elsewhere in S.P.'s empire. The P-11 class, for example (engines 3100-3109) went to the Northwestern Pacific in 1938. Two of them, the 3104 and 3109, were later leased to Southern Pacific of Mexico along with several 2400s. Eight of these latter 2400s were finally sold in 1951 to the Mexican Government, becoming Ferrocarril del Pacifico 300-307. (See the Appendix for details.)

Four engines from the Texas Lines were leased to the Pacific Lines in 1953 (600, 602, 605, and 606) and retained their T&NO numbers. And T&NO 616 (originally 926) is reported to have worked on the Union Pacific for several months in 1913 prior to coming south.

All three of the major American builders of locomotives (American, Baldwin, and Lima) were represented on S.P.'s Pacific roster, as was the railroad's own erecting hall at Sacramento. Baldwin built the most (109) and Lima and Sacramento the fewest (two each).

If the Pacifics' forte when new was the ability to sustain high speeds over long hauls, in later years other traits assured their usefulness to their owner. Good acceleration qualities plus development of ample initial tractive effort made them suitable for the frequent stop, high-performance schedules of the Bay Area commute runs. A number of Pacifics were equipped with trailing truck boosters which helped greatly in this start-stop service.

When the end came to S.P. steam in the late 1950s, most of the Pacifics had served at least 30 years; many were in their 40s, approaching 50. Longevity of this kind in a machine subjected to literally millions of miles of use speaks well for the designers and operators of Southern Pacific's 4-6-2s. A view of the life and times of these engines is depicted in the album that follows, so come along and see what evolved as a high point in the development of S.P. steam. . . .

Previous page: Photograph at Sacramento by David Joslyn.
James E. Boynton collection

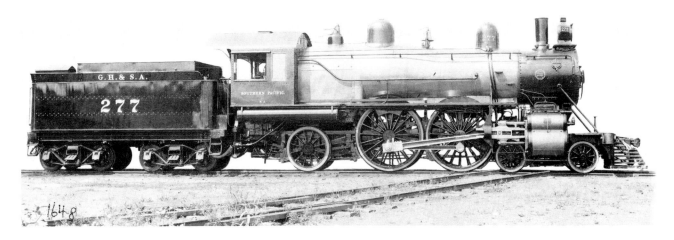

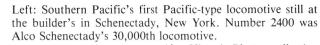

Left: Southern Pacific's first Pacific-type locomotive still at the builder's in Schenectady, New York. Number 2400 was Alco Schenectady's 30,000th locomotive.
Alco Historic Photos collection

Above: The Pacifics' immediate precursors in the evolutionary chain were the Atlantics, some of which were still under construction when the first 4-6-2 types arrived on the property.
Kenneth G. Johnsen collection

Opposite: Within a year after it was introduced into service, the 2405 was pulling a Vanderbilt tender with an oil bunker.
Arnold S. Menke collection

Top: Number 2412 was built new as an oil burner. The Baldwin is shown on the turntable at Sacramento around 1906.
Arnold S. Menke collection

Above: Several of the initial Baldwin Pacifics were built as coal burners. With oil being more plentiful in the West than coal, Southern Pacific standardized its Pacific Lines on oil fuel in the early 1900s. Pacifics such as 2405 were soon re-equipped as oil burners. *James E. Boynton collection*

Opposite bottom: The P-1 through P-5 classes were straight-boilered locomotives. The straight, uncluttered lines of these engines contrasted with the later "wagon top" boilers of the P-6 through P-14 classes. Photo at Ashland, Oregon, in 1910.
James E. Boynton collection

Opposite top: The 2426 stops at Junction City, Oregon, for service about 1910. Tender initials are for Oregon & California Railroad. *James E. Boynton collection*

Top: The 2413 and an Atlantic peek out of the trainshed at the old Arcade Depot in Los Angeles. Note the addition of numberboards astride the smokebox near the smokestacks of both engines. This feature became standard on virtually all S.P. steam locomotives. *Robert B. McNeel collection*

Above: Side-mounted air pump and ample air reservoir are seen in this left side view of 2422 at Woodburn, Oregon, about 1913. *James E. Boynton collection*

Opposite below: The gradual modernization of the early Pacifics is seen in this view of Number 2407 at Sparks, Nevada, in 1917. Relocation of air reservoirs, boiler tube pilot, and Vanderbilt tender are obvious external differences.
Walt Grande collection

Left: Brand-new 2460 basks in the sun at its builder's Sacramento roundhouse in April of 1918. Blue-green boiler and cylinder jackets were commonplace on S.P. power during this era.
James E. Boynton collection

Below: Freight service in Oregon with the 2422.
Walt Grande collection

Opposite below: All decked out for the Third Liberty Loan Special Train is S.P.-built 2460 at West Oakland Yard Office in 1918.

Ted Wurm photo from the collection of James E. Boynton

Opposite top: When World War I cut into the availability of new locomotives from the commercial builders, Southern Pacific augmented its Pacific fleet with two home-built units. Sacramento-built 2459 is as handsome as anything that ever rolled out of Baldwin's erecting hall.

James E. Boynton collection

Above: Ten heavier Pacifics also came with the El Paso & Southwestern and 162 is an example of these hefty coal burners. It became S.P. 3122. *James E. Boynton collection*

Left: El Paso & Southwestern 4-6-2 Number 140 became Southern Pacific Number 3100 and acquired a smokebox-door-mounted headlight. At the time this photo was snapped in the mid-1920s, the engine still burned coal and the steps from pilot beam to runningboard were in the form of a ladder. Both of these features would soon change.

Walt Grande collection

Left below: Ten lightweight Pacifics built for the El Paso & Southwestern in 1907 came to Southern Pacific with the absorption of that road in 1924. EP&SW Number 144 is an example of the type. It became S.P. Number 3104.

Arnold S. Menke collection

Above: Backhead view of S.P. 3128 at the builder's. Enginemen didn't particularly like the P-12s because of their rough riding characteristics. Their high-mounted cabs added further to the shaky feeling. *Alco Historic Photos collection*

Opposite top: Builder's photo of El Paso & Southwestern 168 in 1917. In 1924 this engine became Southern Pacific 3128. This P-12 class was one of the more powerful classes of Pacifics on the S.P. *Alco Historic Photos collection*

Opposite below: Southern Pacific's Texas subsidiary, the Texas & New Orleans, stabled a roster of Pacifics which closely resembled their Pacific Lines counterparts. P-5 Number 901 was renumbered in May of 1923 to Number 601. Photo was taken at Welch, Louisiana, by H. Hill in April 1919. *Arnold S. Menke collection*

Above: Several years of Harriman ownership of both Southern Pacific and Union Pacific evolved some standardized designs. Even the T&NO locomotives showed that influence. Number 921 (later renumbered to 611) came with the typical Harriman extended smokebox. Photo about 1914.

Arnold S. Menke collection

Top: The T&NO P-9 class, though slightly heavier, looked just like the standard Pacific Lines P-10 class. But note the wooden pilot! It was not long before the 629 got the standard boiler tube pilot. Photo by T. Taber in January of 1925.

Arnold S. Menke collection

Right: This train, shown at Third and Townsend Station in San Francisco in 1924, originated in New Orleans. For a time the *Sunset Limited* ran beyond Los Angeles, all the way to San Francisco. The 2485 was destined in later years to become a streamlined Pacific for the *San Joaquin*.

James H. Harrison collection

Above: Smokebox front hinges on the right-hand side do not mar the appealing lines of P-5 Number 600 at San Antonio, Texas, in September of 1937.   *James E. Boynton collection*

Top: Boxpok center drivers were applied to some of the T&NO Pacifics. The 620 at Houston on November 29, 1947, is an example of one such conversion.
Stan Kistler photo from the collection of James H. Harrison

Opposite page: The T&NO Pacifics were practically indistinguishable from their Pacific Lines cousins, with a few exceptions. The date and location of this posed photograph have been lost, but the well-manicured line is probably in West Texas sometime in the 1920s.   *Arnold S. Menke collection*

Left: T&NO 4-6-2s Numbers 614 and 619 sported Elesco feedwater heaters on their brows. The 614 is shown at Dallas on July 31, 1935.   *Arnold S. Menke collection*

Above: *Sunset Limited* hustling out of Beaumont, Texas, in the charge of Pacific 617. Flat lands encouraged speeding and some of the engineers got reputations for "not pulling them down for the curves" just for the fun of showing off.
                    Mac Gaddis photo

Right: Much rebuilt P-9 Number 629 at Houston presents an interesting comparison with an earlier photo of this engine on page 24. Only the T&NO engines received six-axle, semi-Vanderbilt tenders such as this one, and only the P-13s were delivered from the builder with them.

James H. Harrison collection

Above: By the time this view of 614 was snapped in June of 1953, the Elesco feedwater heater was gone and so was the engine's distinctive appearance.   *Arnold S. Menke collection*

Opposite top: The daily New Orleans to San Antonio train, the *Alamo,* stops at Orange, Texas, in July of 1946. The 612 and its string of Harriman passenger cars personify a mode of public intercity transportation that has not been seen in this country for several decades.   *Mac Gaddis photo*

Opposite bottom: P-13s, built in 1928, were the heaviest of all the S.P. Pacifics. They usually only pulled freight on break-in runs. Hoggers didn't like to run these "big engines" into sidings. Former T&NO telegrapher Harold Vollrath remembers a near head-on collision between Number 8 and a P-13 on a freight whose engineer momentarily forgot that he had to take the siding for the passenger train.

A.W. Roberts photo at Ysleta, Texas, on March 1, 1953, from the collection of A.D. McLennan

Right: Backhead of P-13 Number 631.
Railroad Museum of Pennsylvania collection

Above: Pacific Number 2475 on the *Senator* meets the streamlined *Cascade* in 1956 at Martinez where the Overland and Cascade Routes come together with the back-door route from the San Joaquin Valley. *James H. Harrison collection*

Opposite top: Factory-fresh P-8 2461 demonstrates the S.P. Pacifics' presence on the Overland Route, pulling the *San Francisco Overland* across the Lucin Cutoff on Great Salt Lake. The mighty 4-6-2s racked up impressive endurance records between Ogden and Sparks. *James H. Harrison collection*

Opposite bottom: Pacifics hauled the *Coast Daylight* (or *Daylight Limited,* as it was called in its infancy) from its beginning in 1922 until the early 1930s when 4-8-2 locomotives took over. The 2483 has the San Francisco-bound pearl gray train gathering speed through Burbank, California, in May of 1931. Pearl gray, inaugurated in 1930, gave way to red and orange on this train in 1937. *Ted Wurm collection*

Below right: During World War II the *Noon Daylight* was discontinued and the *San Joaquin Daylight* received some of its streamlined equipment. At war's end, the *Noon Daylight* was reinstated and the *San Joaquin* went back to heavyweight equipment. It ran as seen in this photo until 1949, when the *Noon Daylight* was abolished and the *San Joaquin* received all-streamlined equipment.　　　*James E. Boynton collection*

Right: World War II brought changes such as shields over locomotive headlights and restrictions on photography. Photographer Bill Bassler recalls that the day he took this picture of a Pacific-and-caboose hop in Alhambra, a woman yelled out, "He's got a camera!" Soon a policeman was patrolling the area and Bill quit taking train pictures for the duration of the war.

Opposite bottom: Number 71 was the westbound *Daylight Limited* until the time of the streamlined *Coast Daylight*, at which time 71 became the local train. The 2489 has the pearl gray *Daylight Limited* at Santa Barbara during the glory days of that train in 1930.

　　　Tom Taber photo from Arnold Menke collection

Above: Different faces: P-5 Number 2448 and P-11 Number 3108 in their wartime dress illustrate the dissimilarities between the S.P. and EP&SW engines. The pair rubbed shoulders at Santa Barbara in October of 1942.

Photo by Robert B. McNeel

Opposite top: The 2474 has a troop train in the siding at Cordelia, California, presumably from Hamilton Field near San Rafael. War was closer than anyone realized on the day Ted Wurm snapped this photo: December 5, 1941.

Opposite center: Doubleheaded Pacifics roll a cattle train near San Jose in November of 1946. *Wilbur Whittaker photo from the collection of James H. Harrison*

Opposite bottom: The 2432 splits the semaphores at Salem, Oregon, in 1949 with a long freight train and a hobo who apparently likes riding downwind from cattle cars.

Al Augenstein photo from the collection of Tom Gray

Opposite bottom: Piggyback and container trains are nothing new to circus folk. Foley & Burke shows pulled into Tracy in 1939 behind Pacific 2444.   *Tom Gray collection*

Opposite top: Engine crews didn't like using Pacifics on locals. The high-drivered passenger engines slipped too much on little used spurs and side tracks. Number 2437 was photographed in 1943 on the Oxnard local, pulling out of the ice house siding at Santa Barbara, by Robert B. McNeel.

Above: Doubleheaded and working hard: A pair of P-8 class Pacifics combine their power to move this freight train up the grade from Martinez to Carquinez in 1955. Cab-forwards usually worked this grade, but when power was short, even the passenger engines were called.   *Fred Matthews photo*
from the collection of James H. Harrison

Opposite below: The familiar clock tower of Portland's Union Station serves as a backdrop for the 2462 on a clear sunny day in 1937. Engines used in Oregon were sometimes equipped with pilot plows because of the high mountain snow conditions they encountered in the Cascades and Siskiyous.

James E. Boynton photo

Opposite top: Freshly shopped and shiny, booster-equipped 2487 lugs a freight train near Manteca, California, in 1947. Sure hope that sagging reefer behind the tender doesn't yield to the strain!   *James H. Harrison collection*

Above: The P-11s were lightweight, and not well suited for heavy trains. It is unusual, therefore, to find the 3101 unassisted at the head of a freight drag at Indio, California, in this 1947 photo by Mac Gaddis.

Above: Pacifics made their homes at shops associated with passenger service. Santa Barbara roundhouse was one such place. One of the straight-boilered Pacifics is getting ready for the 8:30 A.M. passenger local to Los Angeles in the quiet days just before the outbreak of World War II.

Robert B. McNeel photo

Opposite top: Another busy passenger engine terminal was Mission Bay in San Francisco. Only two Pacifics are seen in this 1948 view; the others are hustling commute trains up and down the peninsula. *Southern Pacific photo from James H. Harrison collection*

Opposite below: San Jose, at the other end of the peninsula from Mission Bay was another 4-6-2 hot spot. The 2471 chuffs past the roundhouse and big brother 4-8-2 Number 4360 in this 1953 photo by Mac Gaddis.

Left center: Whaleback tenders were preferred by engineers in switching service because of their better visibility. The 3109, parked next to a whaleback tender at Taylor roundhouse, was probably never actually coupled to it. Most experts agree: Pacifics did not use whaleback tenders. Bill Bassler took the photo on January 30, 1949.

Opposite below: For every rule, there seems to be an exception. The Pacifics did not use whaleback tenders in regular service, but the engine in this photo is not in regular service. The 2458 was retired on November 15, 1955, and vacated from the roster. An engine was then needed for stationary boiler service in Calexico, so the 2458 was resurrected, fitted with a whaleback tender from a 4-6-0, and sent to Calexico on December 27, 1955. It is shown here at Taylor roundhouse in a rare photo by H.F. Stewart from the collection of Stan Kistler.

Left: Those were the days! With steam locomotive tenders peeking out of every available stall, San Jose roundhouse bedded down a number of Pacifics. Mac Gaddis took this photo in 1955 when time was starting to run out for steam.

Left bottom: Freight Extra 3250 West and train Number 243, pulled by Pacific 2485, leave the huge Sacramento complex at approximately the same time on March 16, 1947.
J.C. Hammond photo from the collection of Walt Grande

Below: P-10 Number 2487 on an Extra East thunders through Elmhurst, California, on October 13, 1956.
Bob Searle photo from the collection of James E. Boynton

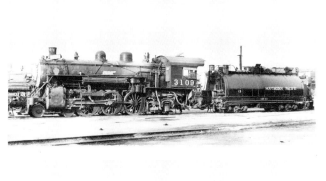

Opposite bottom: Heavy Pacific and heavy Mountain, both skyline casing equipped, team up on the *Owl* on November 2, 1946.

L.L. Bonney photo from the collection of Harre Demoro

Opposite center: The *Sacramento Daylight* was frequently the domain of the Pacifics, although everything from high-drivered Atlantics to GS class 4-8-4s were used on it at one time or another. Photo at Lathrop in March of 1955, where the *Sacramento* and *San Joaquin Daylights* met. The 2486 was one of the three P-10s originally streamlined for the *San Joaquin Daylight*. The skirting and bright colors had long since been removed by the time of this photo, however.

Guy L. Dunscomb photo from the collection of James E. Boyton

Opposite top: For a number of years in the '40s, train Number 71 acted as a local between Los Angeles and Santa Barbara. It transferred passengers to Number 99 at Santa Barbara where the *Daylight* ran around it. This photo was taken by Robert B. McNeel in 1949. At that time the *Coast Daylight* was not yet dieselized: however, diesel power from the Sunset or Golden State Routes occasionally was put on 99 at Los Angeles.

Above: This photo (by James E. Boynton on February 21, 1937) shows the 2491 at Sacramento looking quite "as-built" save for the tender.

In this later view of 2491 (by Guy Dunscomb on February 28, 1948, from James E. Boynton collection) the skyline casing is the most obvious change, but sharp-eyed Pacific spotters will notice many other subtle changes as well.

Opposite below: The two Lima-built Pacifics that originally operated on the Arizona Eastern wound up their days in the Bay Area. Number 2477 is in commuter service at Third and Townsend in July 1953.   *James H. Harrison collection*

Opposite top: Skyline casings were introduced on the S.P. by GS-2 4-8-4 *Daylight* locomotives in 1936. S.P. liked the idea and applied them to a number of Pacifics and Mountains at a number of their own shops. Differences in design, bell placement, etc., are illustrated in this photo taken by Arthur Lloyd at Sacramento on March 30, 1952.

Top: The 2482 passes through Roseville yards on June 4, 1950, with Number 202, the San Francisco–Gerber train.
     Wilbur C. Whittaker photo

Left: Number 2491 has a long string of coaches in tow as it leaves Oakland with a Big Game Rooters' Special on November 22, 1947.   *Fred Matthews photo from the collection of James H. Harrison*

Above: Los Gatos-bound: Lima-built 2476 and train turn off the S.P. main at California Avenue in Palo Alto. Photo on August 28, 1955, by Mac Gaddis.

Opposite top: In this bucolic scene at Vasona Junction, California, in 1954, the 2476 is pulling an excursion of the Northern California Railroad Club to Los Gatos.
    Bob Searle photo from the collection of James E. Boynton

Opposite below: Engines on the Los Altos branch could not be turned around, so a backup boiler-tube pilot was applied to the tender of Number 2476. This engine was usually used to pull the Los Gatos commute trains.   *Mac Gaddis photo*

Right: Spruced up P-8 Number 2475 was the last S.P. Pacific to operate under steam (on a New Year's Day, 1958 excursion). It is shown at West Oakland in 1956.   *Ted Wurm collection*

Right center: 4-6-2 Number 2481 was the last Pacific to receive a skyline casing (in 1948) and is seen in this pleasing portrait by Doug Richter on September 2, 1952, at San Francisco.
    From the collection of James E. Boynton

Above: To the bystander, the man in the cab had a place of honor and importance. He was in control of the powerful black machine stretched out before him. The fireman on Number 248, the *El Dorado* at Martinez in the summer of '53, is probably not pondering his importance as much as how soon he will be able to tie up and get out of that hot cab.

Robert A. Campbell photo

Opposite top: Look what's passing overhead as the 2469 clanks along the Vacaville branch on September 25, 1949: It's a Sacramento Northern interurban, complete with open-platform trailer car. *Wilbur C. Whittaker photo*

Opposite below: This scene may be repeated with the resurrection of the 2472. Here the future celebrity is wheeling Number 248, the San Francisco–Sacramento train, on June 30, 1941.

Wilbur C. Whittaker photo

Opposite below: Future Cinderella engine 2472 gallops along near Palo Alto on August 28, 1955.   *Mac Gaddis photo*

Opposite top: Train time at Sacramento in the late '40s.
    Earl Fancher photo from the collection of Harre Demoro

Top: The 2468 and train Number 55 pass freight extra X1771 stopped at Merced, California, on a warm and sunny July 2, 1946.   *Ted Wurm photo*

Right: In an effort to improve visibility and working space for enginemen, the cabs of some Pacifics were replaced with so-called "sport cabs" and moved slightly further back on the locomotive. The 2464 exemplifies this alteration.
    Arnold S. Menke collection

Opposite below: Alco Brooks 4-6-2 2454 leaving Oakland's 16th Street Station for the Mole in 1940 presents quite a contrast from the view of the same engine in the previous photo.
James E. Boynton collection

Opposite top: A time-honored pose of P-6 (American-built) 2454 in action. The location is Gilroy, California, and the date is 1953.
Robert C. Myers photo
from the collection of Kenneth G. Johnsen

Top: Some of the S.P. Pacifics that went south left their bones in Mexico. Number 304, the former 2439, is seen partly dismantled at Empalme shops on February 25, 1956.
A.M. Paine photo

Right: A number of S.P. Pacifics made their way into Mexico. Number 2452 is pulling the Tucson-Nogales *Mexican Express* in 1950 along a weed-grown right-of-way.
Wilbur C. Whittaker photo

Opposite bottom: This view by Wilbur C. Whittaker, looking down on a troop train rounding San Pablo Bay, shows an interesting mix of G.I. sleepers and heavyweight Pullmans, as well as a good look at the details on the top of 2440's boiler. Pinole, California, on March 3, 1946.

Opposite center: The 2451, just out of the Los Angeles shop on December 24, 1922, receives the shop crew's finishing touches. The boiler and cylinder jackets are painted blue-green. This was a common feature on many S.P. locomotives at this time. Modern-day restorers of the 2472 found a hidden spot next to its boiler which had blue-green paint on the back side, giving rise to the theory that it too was once painted this way. *T. Taber photo from the collection of Arnold S. Menke*

Opposite top: Jim Boynton snapped this fine portrait of the 2444 at Oakland in 1936. Everyone has their preferences and straight-boilered machines such as this one are Boynton's favorites.

Top left: Pacific 2452 in freight service at Hermosillo, Mexico, on April 6, 1952. *Arnold S. Menke collection*

Top right: With the Sierras and the Nevada deserts behind it, the *Overland,* pulled by double-headed P-5s, stops at West Berkeley on August 4, 1937.
L.L. Bonney photo from the collection of Harre Demoro

Above right: Extra 2433 East consists of a straight-boilered P-3 and a heavyweight private car. The Pacifics could be entrusted with all types of service. West Oakland yard on December 7, 1939. *Robert Searle photo from the collection of James E. Boynton*

Left: Herbert Hoover's campaign special in 1928 has spotless 2489 for its motive power.
S.P. photo from James H. Harrison collection

Above: A highway bridge now parallels this railroad bridge across the Carquinez Straights (of the Sacramento River). Pacific Number 2422 clattered off the bridge north of Martinez in 1936. *Walt Grande collection*

Opposite top: Southern Pacific's second Pacific helps the *Pacific Limited* at West Oakland on May 18, 1941.
L.L. Bonney photo from the collection of Harre Demoro

Opposite below: Pacifics were frequently employed as passenger train helpers in later years. Here the 2420 joins a GS-4 on the *San Joaquin Daylight* at Bakersfield for the climb over Tehachapi. Fireman Bob McNeel photographed the action in September 1941.

Opposite below: From pilot plows to footboards, Pacifics in Oregon presented a variety of interesting faces. Number 2407 at Grant's Pass, Oregon, on July 9, 1949, looks almost like a switcher on the irregular track.   *Arthur L. Lloyd photo*

Opposite top: Four engines and 99 cars working near Alhambra in January 1942. Pacific 3123 leads Mogul 1742, Pacific 2443, and Mikado 3236.   *Robert L. Kern collection*

Above: Steam from 2415's booster engine envelops its tender and headend car at San Jose, California, September 14, 1941.
Kenneth G. Johnsen collection

Right: The *Daylight Limited* (an early version of the *Coast Daylight)* operated as train Nos. 71 and 72. Upon inauguration of the *Coast Daylight* as trains 98 and 99, the local passenger train from Los Angeles to Santa Barbara was assigned the numbers 71 and 72. The 2418 does the honors on the very first day of operation of the local as No. 71, February 16, 1936.
Photo by Robert B. McNeel

Opposite below: Built by Baldwin in 1907 for the El Paso & Southwestern, dapper little 3109 was taken into the Southern Pacific fold in 1924 when the big road absorbed the EP&SW. The engine was still looking pretty spiffy when Jim Boynton took this photo at Mission Bay in 1936.

Above: Football specials to Palo Alto crowd the tracks at Third and Townsend in San Francisco. No fewer than eight Pacifics and one Ten Wheeler squeezed into this 1933 photo from the collection of Harre Demoro.

Right: The P-11 class was among the oldest and lightest of S.P.'s Pacifics and was leased to subsidiary Northwestern Pacific for three years beginning in 1938. Here, Number 3100 is ready to depart Santa Rosa on NWP in 1938.
Waldemar Sievers photo from the collection of Harre Demoro

Opposite bottom: Husky hauler: don't let 3123's footboards and puny excursion train fool you; the P-12 class was among the heaviest and most powerful Pacifics on the system. Photo is at Lodi in March of 1952, from the camera of Mac Gaddis.

Opposite top: Crossing tender holds traffic as former EP&SW 4-6-2 3106 leaves San Jose, bound for San Francisco in 1930.
Ted Wurm collection

Top: Unlike their lightweight P-11 cousins, the P-12 Pacifics were put to work in mainline service everywhere on the system. Here, the 3120 (former EP&SW 160) erupts a cloud of black smoke as it moves No. 14, the *Pacific Limited,* out of the 16th Street station in Oakland. *James E. Boynton collection*

Right: The hand-me-downs from El Paso, with their choppy, shortened look, were not in the same esthetically pleasing class with say, a Pacific Lines P-8 or P-10. And the high cab was definitely disliked by the enginemen it jostled during high-speed running. This picture gives an interesting look at tender size, however; it is somewhat reminiscent of erstwhile Pennsylvania Railroad engines with their huge tender-to-engine size ratios. *James H. Harrison collection*

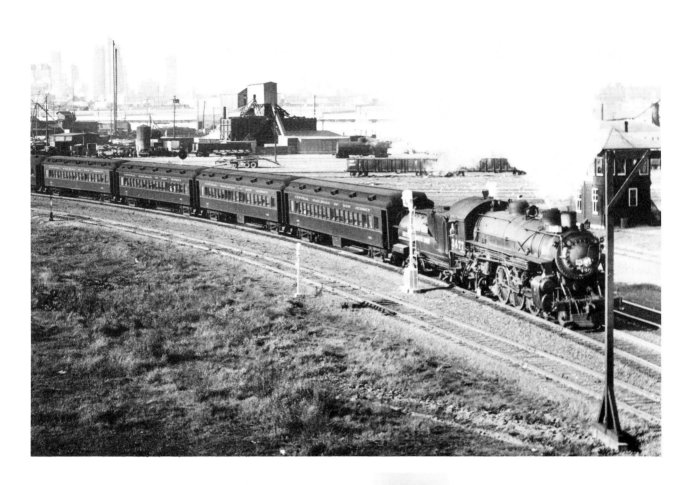

Opposite bottom: The commuter pool was the melting pot as well as the last stand for various classes of S.P. steam, including the Pacifics. Here, in late 1956 a former *Daylight* GS-4 bids farewell to Lima-built 2477 pulling out of the station. Although steam-powered commute trains vanished in January of 1957, the dependable 2477 was not officially vacated from S.P.'s roster until September 24, 1958. *Photo by Mac Gaddis*

Opposite top: What's this, the Central Railroad of New Jersey in San Francisco? During World War II the War Production Board transferred about twenty CNJ coaches to S.P. lease. The reason was increased commuter demand owing to high production at Bethlehem Shipyard facilities in San Francisco and South San Francisco. Trusty 2477 heads south with a string of them. In early 1946 all twenty cars were returned.
Arthur L. Lloyd photo

Above: Commute service consisted of relatively short trains on a fast start-stop schedule. Booster-equipped 2487 was the ideal motive power for such an application. Making its brief stop at Redwood City on April 25, 1953, the 2487 will momentarily begin its rapid acceleration out of town, only to be followed soon after by another trainload of commuters.
Arthur L. Lloyd photo

Above: The sands have just about run out for the 2476 in this final view of it pouring out heavy oil smoke in suburban San Francisco on October 2, 1956. Within a couple months its voice would be stilled forever.　　*Arnold S. Menke collection*

Opposite top: The evening rush hour began with a lineup of trains at Third and Townsend in San Francisco. Commuters getting off work would hurry to catch the train that was going to make a stop closest to their home. The trains would whistle out of San Francisco at speed and the parade began. Something similar in concept still leaves San Francisco at rush hour today, but the modern F-40 diesel and stainless steel coaches somehow have failed to capture the author's imagination the way the handsome trains in this photo did.　　*Waldemar Sievers photo from the collection of Harre Demoro*

Opposite bottom: How will S.P. Pacifics be remembered? Old-timers of course will visualize the classic Fred Jukes shots of the 4-6-2 drawn *Overland Limited* flying across Nevada under a billowing plume. Younger generations will probably remember the handsome smaller engines that shared the honors with their larger MT and GS brethren on the Bay Area commute runs.　　*S.P. photo from James H. Harrison collection*

The Streamliners

STREAMLINING CAME OF AGE in the decade of the 1930s. A nation trying to crawl out of its worst-yet depression looked for positive signs that better times would return. The transportation industry responded in part with the introduction of lighter weight, speedier (read less wind-resistant) trains whose amenities invited the public to ride the rails again.

Southern Pacific can rightfully lay claim to the most famous post-depression streamliner, the million-dollar red and orange Daylight. S.P. was not alone in the streamliner business, however. In fact, in Texas the pioneering effort of one of Southern Pacific's arch rivals stimulated S.P. to launch a scaled-down Texas version of the Daylight.

Texans, it must be understood, have a penchant for doing things their own way. Streamlined passenger trains were no exception. When the Burlington Route inaugurated its *Sam Houston Zephyr* on October 1, 1936, the S.P.'s Texas subsidiary Texas & New Orleans was challenged to do something to protect its share of the Dallas–Houston traffic.

Daylight 4-8-4s with 16 cars were not appropriate for the shorter, less heavily traveled Dallas–Houston run, so the T&NO leased (and later purchased outright) three P-6 Pacifics from parent S.P. and transformed them in their Houston shops. The three, S.P. 2455, 2456, and 2457 would become T&NO 650, 651, and 652 respectively.

In the rebuild, the trio got Boxpok drivers and their boiler pressure was raised from 200 to 210 pounds. T&NO wanted them to be capable of 100 miles per hour, although the top speed of the run was only 80. Several thousand pounds of shrouding was added to reduce wind resistance and give a streamlined appearance.

Skirting and skyline casings similar to those of the Daylights were applied. A streamlined shroud supported by a solid pilot with hidden front coupler sloped up to a conical silver bullet nose.

The Pacifics' Vanderbilt tenders did not have streamlining added. The engines and tenders, however, were painted in a red, orange, black, and silver paint scheme just like the one their Daylight sisters wore in California and they were given matching streamlined cars. The rebuilt 4-6-2 speedsters were reclassified P-14. The first one was completed in July of 1937 and the other two followed in August. They entered service on September 19, 1937.

These "Texas Daylights," as some have called them, pulled the flagship of the Dallas–Houston run, the non-stop *Sunbeam.* They also hauled the *Hustler,* stopping for local passengers along the way. Two trainsets operated each day, going one way as the *Sunbeam* and the other way as the *Hustler.*

T&NO's streamlined Pacifics chalked up 16 years of dependable service—this on top of the 24 years they had already worked as run-of-the-mill plain black 4-6-2s on the Pacific Lines.

In California, Southern Pacific's San Joaquin Valley Route was growing in importance. S.P. had begun *San Joaquin Flyer* service in 1927 with conventional equipment. When, in 1941, new equipment purchases for the streamlined *Coast Daylight* freed up some of its first-generation streamlined equipment, the time was ripe to upgrade the *San Joaquin.*

As with the Texas trains, the *San Joaquin* was not thought to be heavily enough patronized to warrant the full 4-8-4 treatment. With the exception of the climb over Tehachapi, most of the San Joaquin Valley Line was fairly level running.

Pacifics, once again, were turned to as the logical midsized motive power appropriate for this run. Three of the newest, booster-equipped models on the roster, P-10s, were selected for what was to become the *San Joaquin Daylight.* They were the 2484, 2485, and 2486.

The engines were sent to the Los Angeles Shops where a facelift was performed. Skyline casing smoke lifters had already been applied to several other Pacifics and the *San Joaquins* now got them too. In addition, a skirt resembling that of a GS Northern was applied. Pilot and smokebox front remained unstreamlined as built, however.

The engines and tenders were painted in the tried-and-true scheme of red, orange, black, and silver in stripes to match the other Daylight equipment. The 2485 inaugurated the *San Joaquin Daylight* on July 4, 1941.

Page 70: Texas *Daylight*. Paint hasn't yet been applied to *Sunbeam* Number 651 as it is spun around on the Dallas turntable following its first shakedown run from Houston. More streamlined than its Pacific Lines cousins, this Houston rebuild sports a shroud between pilot beam and bullet nose and a concealed front coupler. The date is August 12, 1937.

Harold K. Vollrath collection

Previous page: Smart looking T&NO Number 650 is a tribute to the skills of the Houston shop forces. Inspiration for the streamlining treatment came from the Pacific Lines' GS-2 4-8-4 *Daylight* engines which were introduced about five months earlier. *Stan Kistler photo from collection of James H. Harrison*

War clouds came in a few months and it wasn't long before the San Joaquin 4-6-2s lost their colorful paint scheme. As did their GS sisters, the streamlined Pacifics became all-black and sported hooded visors over their headlights and all other lights. Enemy pilots were not supposed to be able to see a black, visored engine as easily as one that had some red and orange paint splashed on the side of it.

Discontinuance in 1942 of the *Noon Daylight* on the Coast Route provided a windfall of additional streamlined passenger equipment for the *San Joaquin Daylight*. However, easy come–easy go. In 1946, after war's end, the *Noon Daylight* was reinstated and the *San Joaquin Daylight* had to be content with a mix of older standard equipment and some new stock.

The need for flashy red and orange stripes on the Pacifics seemed to have gone, and so they remained black. In 1950 they lost their skirting. From that date on, they served the rest of their careers looking much like their other P-10 sisters.

Postwar increases in traffic eventually led to the replacement of the Pacifics on the *San Joaquin Daylight* with larger 4-8-2 and 4-8-4 locomotives.

Opposite below: The third of the three Pacifics acquired by T&NO in 1937, S.P. 2457 is seen at Oakland on August 16, 1935.
Guy L. Dunscomb photo from James E. Boynton collection

Opposite top: Besides a larger tender, some of the improvements applied by the Houston shops included Boxpok drivers, new trailer truck and "sport" cab. The 651, formerly the 2456, is shown at Dallas on August 12, 1937, following completion of its first shakedown run. Next comes the red, orange, black and silver paint.   *Harold K. Vollrath collection*

Top: S.P. 4-6-2 Number 2456 was the only engine of the *Sunbeam* trio that arrived at Houston equipped with a feedwater heater. During the rebuild, all three engines were to receive them. The handsome Pacific is shown here at Oakland on October 24, 1936.   *James E. Boynton photo*

Right: The future T&NO Number 650 as it looked at Oakland a few months before its transformation. It is a typical workhorse P-6. Photo date: December 29, 1936.
James E. Boynton photo

Opposite below: It is June 1953, and just out of Houston train 13, the northbound *Sunbeam,* is flying along faster than the cars on the adjacent highway. Streamlined Pacific Number 650 will return on tomorrow morning's *Hustler.*
Harold K. Vollrath collection

Opposite top: Northbound No. 15, the *Hustler,* is shown at Bremond, Texas, on March 8, 1947. This was one of the numerous passenger stops between Houston and Dallas made by the *Hustler,* counterpart to the nonstop *Sunbeam.*
Arnold S. Menke collection

Above: Their extra-tall skyline casings gave the P-14s an appearance that was distinct from their *Daylight* cousins on the West Coast. The look was patterned after the *Daylight,* however, right down to the *Sunbeam* script lettering on the engine's skirt.
James H. Harrison collection

Left: Looking the way a streamlined Pacific ought to look, T&NO Number 652 (the former 2457) shows off its racy lines in Dallas in April of 1940. Even if the reduced wind resistance didn't offset the several thousand pounds of added shroud weight, the pleasing appearance was bound to have a beneficial effect on patronage. *Harold K. Vollrath collection*

Above: The *Sunbeam* P-14s dashed back and forth between Dallas and Houston for 16 years before being stricken from the roster and replaced by Alco PAs. Photo at South Dallas in March of 1948 from the Harold K. Vollrath collection.

Opposite top: Looking the worse for wear, Number 652 is seen in 1952 near the end of its days. The door concealing the front coupler has been opened so the battered Pacific could be shunted about by a switcher. *John Fink photo from the collection of the California State Railroad Museum*

Opposite below: Busy Pacifics of the *Sunbeam–Hustler* run were on the road over ten hours a day between Dallas and Houston. Photo is at Dallas in the spring of 1939, from the collection of Harold K. Vollrath.

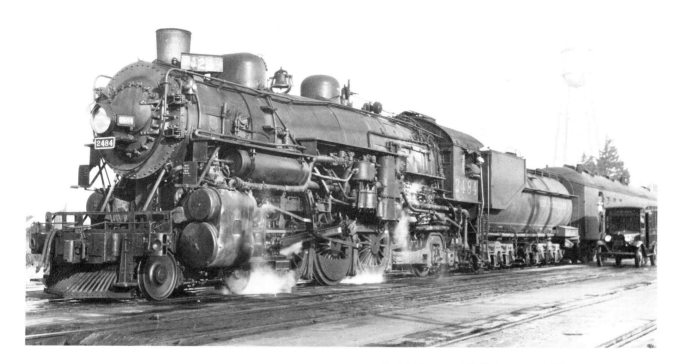

Opposite below: Lack of streamlined pilot or bullet nose gave the San Joaquins a sort of hybrid appearance. 1947 photo from the collection of James H. Harrison.

Opposite top: Handsome P-10 4-6-2s were dolled up for the *San Joaquin Daylight* in 1941. Shroud was limited to skirting and skyline casing. Photo at Bakersfield, California, in September of 1941 by Robert B. McNeel.

Top: Several years prior to its *San Joaquin Daylight* outfitting, Number 2484 was photographed in Berkeley at the head end of the *Owl,* an overnight Pullman train from Los Angeles. Photo date: April 15, 1936.   *James E. Boynton photo*

Above right: The P-10 class was considered by some to be as handsome a locomotive as any ever rostered by the Southern Pacific. The future *Daylight* is seen at Sacramento on October 9, 1938, in a fine portrait by James E. Boynton.

Opposite below: The big day! Freshly shopped 2485 launches the streamlined *San Joaquin Daylight,* No. 52, on July 4, 1941. *L.L. Bonney photo*
from the collection of Harre Demoro

Opposite top: Fresh out of the shops at Los Angeles and ready to inaugurate the streamlined *San Joaquin Daylight,* Number 2485 posed on June 25, 1941. *Arnold S. Menke collection*

Top: Initial run of Number 52 on July 4, 1941, gets under way at West Berkeley. *L.L. Bonney photo*
from the collection of Harre Demoro

Right: Premier trip of the refurbished *San Joaquin Daylight* passing the yard at Tracy on its way to Los Angeles.
J.C. Hammond photo from the collection of Walt Grande

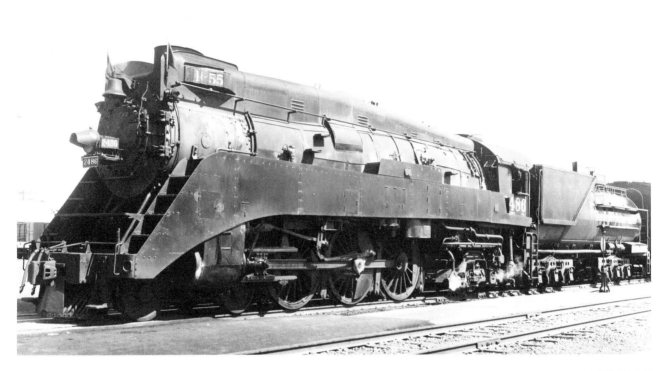

Opposite below: Just a few months after the above photo was taken, this view of 2486 in its *Daylight* dress was made. The bright colors were not to last long on the *San Joaquins*. With the outbreak of World War II just five months after inauguration of the train, S.P. began painting all engines black and applying hoods over all lights to shield them from enemy surveillance.   *Arnold S. Menke collection*

Opposite top: Wartime machine. The 2486 displays the hoods over headlight and classification lamps as well as the somber black paint scheme worn by S.P. steam engines during World War II. Photo at Modesto, California, on March 26, 1944, by Guy L. Dunscomb from the collection of James E. Boynton.

Above: Pre-streamlining view of Number 2486 at Oakland on June 28, 1941.   *Walt Grande collection*

Opposite below: In their final years the streamlined P-10s looked almost like the other skyline casing-equipped P-10s, except for the stairs from the pilot beam to the runningboard. The 2484 acquired one other novel distinguishing feature, a Scullen disc driver. Train is at Lathrop in 1956.
Arnold S. Menke collection

Opposite top: Broadside photo of Number 2485 getting a drink and some lubrication gives a good view of the "sport" cab applied to many of the Pacifics as well as the "humpback" skyline casing applied by the Los Angeles shops. Compare to the Houston version on the *Sunbeam. Waldemar Sievers photo from the collection of Harre Demoro*

Top: With the cessation of hostilities after 1945, S.P. began repainting GS 4-8-4s into their traditional red and orange *Daylight* livery. The P-10s on the *San Joaquin* did not fare so well, however. Their skirting remained black until it was removed altogether in 1950. The 2485 is rolling along near Salida with the Valley Local in 1948.
From the collection of James H. Harrison

Right: Pacific 2484 and the Los Angeles-bound *San Joaquin Daylight* at Emeryville, California, about 1941.
James E. Boynton collection

Tenders

PACIFICS ON THE S.P. used an astonishing variety of tenders over the years, from diminutive to massive, from rectangular to cylindrical. Tender evolution paralleled locomotive evolution.

Southern Pacific classified its tenders according to water capacity and shape. The first numbers used in the classification system were taken from the water capacity, the letter following indicated shape, and the number following that indicated a subsequent variation on the original design. Thus a 120-C-1 was the first 12,000-gallon cylindrical design and a 90-R-4 was the fourth 9,000-gallon rectangular design.

Without its tender a steam locomotive is helplessly incomplete. The same can be said for a book on steam locomotives if it does not include a look at the tenders that were the engines' constant companions. S.P. tender expert Arnold S. Menke deserves the credit for the photos and captions that follow.

Left: The T&NO P-9s came with 12,000-gallon Vanderbilt tenders that were identical to the S.P.'s class 120-C-1 except that the wheel diameter was 36″ instead of 33″. Brakeman's shanties such as the one shown were applied to many T&NO tenders beginning in 1946.

Bob Gray photo from Arnold S. Menke collection

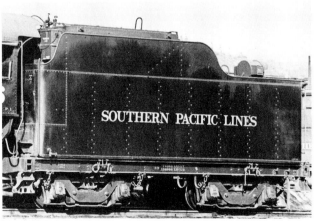

Opposite left bottom: This is an S.P. 160-C-2 tender. With one possible exception*, none of the Pacific Lines 4-6-2s used these large tenders, but the T&NO P-13s came from the factory with them in 1928. The T&NO apparently ordered additional 160-C-2s from Baldwin at that time and assigned them to their P-9s. These were the largest Vanderbilts on the S.P. and the T&NO, holding 16,152 gallons of water. They employed the Commonwealth "water bottom" cast-steel frame.
John Lawson photo from the collection of Arnold S. Menke

For three weeks in 1942, P-10 Number 2484 was assigned a 160-C-3. It is unknown, however, if the combination was in service during that period or simply sitting idle at the shop.

Opposite left center: Photo is at Los Angeles in 1936, showing a 90-R-1 still riding on archbar trucks, looking pretty much as-built. About half of the P-1s came with these tenders, which when new in 1906, were the largest capacity tanks on the S.P. They were the first to come with buffers and vestibules. Evidently the idea was a failure, because by 1920 the S.P. had an active program of removing the buffers and vestibules. Engine 2418 was unusual in that it used the same tender from the mid-twenties until the time of its retirement in 1948. S.P. freely swapped tenders around from one engine to another and at least one engine had as many as 36 tender changes over its career.
*Gerald M. Best photo
from the collection of Arnold S. Menke*

Opposite top: This photo, taken about 1916, shows the appearance of the first five P-1 tenders. By the time this photo had been taken, the side bearing support casting over the front truck had been removed to provide three-point suspension and hence better tracking.
Arnold S. Menke collection

Above: Tenders in the 90-R-7 class were enlarged from 60-R-1s by stretching the water tank, adding a long auxiliary oil tank on top and putting the whole business on top of a new frame. S.P. constructed 50 of these tenders in 1929–1930 and used them on a variety of engines, including the P-11s. Photo date 1947.
J. Lawson photo

Opposite right bottom: The 90-R-6s were former EP&SW tanks and came with the P-12 class. By 1930, however, they were reassigned to other engines, including a few light 2400s. These tenders had six-foot wheelbase pedestal trucks for high-speed service. When new, they had a coal bunker and came equipped with a vestibule. They were converted to oil in 1920–1929, holding a little over 3,300 gallons of fuel. The neatly coiled tubing and associated valves above each truck were used to cool hot journals. Photo date 1939.
*Allan Youell photo
from the collection of Arnold S. Menke*

Opposite right center: An early view of a 90-R-4 showing how the vestibule and buffer were applied to the 9,000-gallon rectangular tenders. Although they were not original equipment with Pacifics, the 90-R-3s and identical 90-R-4s were commonly used behind light 4-6-2s in the twenties, thirties and forties.
*R.P. Middlebrook photo
from the collection of Arnold S. Menke*

Above: Class 90-C-1 in service behind the 2403 in 1947. The 90-C-1s and identical 90-C-2s differed from the 7,000-gallon Vanderbilts in having an extra cylindrical course on the water tank that raised the capacity by 2,000 gallons.
Bob Gray photo from the collection of Arnold S. Menke

Opposite top: The S.P. placed all 9,000-gallon Vanderbilt tenders that had a vestibule in class 90-C-2. This photo is of one that still has the vestibule (minus the buffer) about 1935. Note the track sprinkler, an S.P. innovation, behind the front truck.   *R. Berry photo from Arnold S. Menke collection*

Opposite right center: The first six P-10 Pacifics came from the factory with 120-C-2 tenders such as this one. The most obvious difference between the 120-C-2s and the 120-C-1s is the shape of the truck side frame, with its hump over the journals. These tenders had been exchanged for six-wheel truck tenders on all of the P-10s except one by 1928.
F.C. Smith photo from the collection of Arnold S. Menke

Opposite bottom: The 100-C-3s were built by S.P. starting in 1918. They were stretched 70-Cs. Two cylindrical courses were added to the water tank, apparently between the first and second original courses. With the exception of one week, the tender in this photo stayed with engine 2420 from 1923 to 1951. Photo date 1946.
Bob Gray photo from Arnold S. Menke collection

Opposite left center: The P-8 Pacifics came new with 12,000-gallon Vanderbilt tenders that looked like this 120-C-1. All of the 120-C classes had Commonwealth cast steel frames with integral end sills. By 1929, most of the P-8s were reassigned six-wheel truck tenders.
R. Berry photo from the collection of Arnold S. Menke

Bottom left: Class 120-C-4 consisted of only one tender, Number 8694, the tank that came new with the first 4-10-2, No. 5000. The oil and water tank were the same as in class 120-C-3, but a small deck was added behind the oil tank and was reached from the runningboards via short ladders. Previous 120-C classes had a traditional circular handbrake mounted on the front of the oil tank on the engineer's side. But on the 120-C-4, a Miner Ideal Safety handbrake of the staff type was used. It was mounted on a bracket that stuck up from the left rear of the oil tank. The shaft of the handbrake dropped down through the water tank inside a pipe. This tender spent most of its life behind Pacifics after being removed from the 5000 in 1929. Its final assignment was with P-7 2476. This rear view of the 120-C-4 shows the deck behind the oil tank and the Miner staff type handbrake sticking up in the air. The long flange beneath the words "Southern Pacific" was a splash shield that kept overflow water (during filling of the tank) from getting into the truck journals.   *Collection of Arnold S. Menke*

Center left: Class 120-C-8 was the last group of 12,000-gallon Vanderbilt tenders received by the S.P., and all of them came new with 4-10-2s in 1926. These tenders evolved directly from the 120-C-5 design but had a larger oil tank, an improved truck, and held 12,150 gallons of water. By 1930 all of the 5000s were using 16,000-gallon Vanderbilt tenders exclusively, and the 120-C-8s were assigned to smaller engines, including P-8s, P-10s, and P-12s. The tender shown in this rear view spent its last twenty years with engine 2471.
                Arnold S. Menke collection

Above left: S.P. tender Number 8723, a 120-C-6, was leased to the T&NO with P-6 2455 in 1937. In addition to changing the serial number to 2435, the T&NO made certain other modifications: the 33″ diameter wheels were replaced with 36″ ones, and the oil tank side was extended forward 8-3/8 inches by welding a strip of steel to the front edge as seen in this photo. This minor bit of streamlining was apparently an attempt to minimize visibility of the gangway area.   *C.W. Witbeck photo from the collection of Arnold S. Menke*

Opposite top right: In 1925 and 1926 the S.P. disassembled 23 of their class 120-C-1 tenders. The tanks from these units were then applied to new cast-steel frames mounted on six-wheel trucks. The end result was the class 120-C-6. P-10 Pacific 2485 was streamlined in 1941 and this company photo shows how its 120-C-6 tender end was painted. Note the small backup lamp mounted on the end of the tank. These lights began being applied to S.P. tenders in the late twenties, and some lasted into the late forties. The lower surface of the lamp housed a pair of small lights which illuminated the rear face of the tender. *Arnold S. Menke collection*

Above: The last eight P-10s came with tenders in class 120-C-3. Water and oil tanks were identical to those of the 120-C-2 class, but the Commonwealth cast steel underframe was beefier and it rode on six-wheel Commonwealth trucks. The 44 120-C-3 tenders were commonly used behind the P-8s, P-10s, and a few of the P-12s until the end of steam.
Arnold S. Menke photo

Right: This is one of the original 7,000-gallon semicylindrical tenders that came from Baldwin in 1907 with EP&SW Nos. 144–149. This 1931 view shows the coal bunker after rebuilding by the S.P. for clear vision rearward. One of the most distinctive features of these tenders was the Andrews truck they rolled on. The side frame had an unusually high arch.
T. Taber photo from Arnold S. Menke collection

Off the Rails

FATE PLAYS NO favorites when it comes to train wrecks. Sometimes the newest speedster on the line will hit the ties while much older teakettles plod along for years without ever leaving the rails.

To the enginemen, wrecks are the most fearsome aspect of their jobs. Death by scalding steam while pinned inside the twisted wreckage of a locomotive cab was a nightmare no railroader liked to conjure. To railroad management, wrecks are bad for the balance sheet, bad for public relations, and a legal headache no one in his right mind would want to take on voluntarily.

To the railroad enthusiast and modeler, there is a curious fascination with wrecks. Oh, no one wants them to happen and certainly no one would ever wish death or injury to train crews. But when wrecks do occur, it is something similar to a fire drill at school. All that is normal stops. Order and predictability cease and everything is suddenly topsy-turvy.

Engines and cars built for speed and motion are stopped dead, their faces pushed into the dirt. The once powerful and untouchable iron horse is now mercilessly pushed around by the wrecking crane in a determined effort to get it off the right-of-way so that the line can be rebuilt and opened for service as soon as possible.

Hauled back to the locomotive shops in what is called a hospital train, the wrecked locomotives and cars are appraised and the decision is made to either rebuild them or scrap them.

Big shops such as Southern Pacific's at Los Angeles, Houston, and Sacramento built locomotives from scratch. Consequently they had little difficulty rebuilding even some of the most pathetic basket cases when it could be shown that the cost of the rebuild was lower than the cost of replacement.

Reconstruction could at times be a lengthy process, but the end result was generally a credit to the shop forces who had performed the operation. When a locomotive's useful life was spent, however, the end came quickly. Scrappers with torches could reduce a once-proud locomotive to a pile of scrap metal in a couple of days.

S.P. Pacifics were involved in numerous altercations, photos of which appear on the next few pages. Most survived to run again.

Previous page: In the wreck of the 2458 at Metz, California, in 1916, the engine's Vanderbilt tender turned about-face and ended up sandwiched between the baggage car and locomotive. The Metz wreck was blamed on saboteurs.

Robert B. McNeel collection

Opposite below: Sometimes wrecks afford modelers their best views of underside details. P-1 Number 2426 lies belly-up on an embankment near Santa Margarita in 1912.
Robert B. McNeel collection

Opposite top: One of the most costly disasters, in terms of loss of life, involving a 4-6-2, occurred at Colton, California, on March 28, 1907. Pacific 2416 hit a derail at speed and overturned, with its train piling up behind it. Ten people perished.
Robert B. McNeel collection

Above: Despite the heavy damage inflicted in the Colton wreck, Number 2416 was rebuilt and provided the railroad with another 40 years of service! *Bob Kern collection*

Right: Data is lacking for this photo from James E. Boynton's collection, but it is evident the 2438 collided with the rear end of another passenger train with these disastrous results.

Top: A section crew left a switch lined for the spur at the Kadota Fig Company in Manteca, California, with tragic results. S.P. 2401, at the head of a passenger train, plowed into the siding, jumped the track, and destroyed part of the building. Nevertheless, the 2401 was eventually rebuilt to run again, although it would not be so lucky in a later accident (see page 99, top photo). *James E. Boynton collection*

Opposite bottom left: S.P. 2479, pulling train Number 26, the *Owl,* was derailed by the car of a drunken motorist at Selma, California, on February 12, 1937. Engineer and fireman both died in the crash; the motorist walked away.
James E. Boynton collection

Opposite left center: Everyone turned out on April 10, 1915, to see the results of Number 2434's jumping the track at Gonzales Siding, some 35 miles south of Watsonville Junction.
James E. Boynton collection

Opposite center right: Sideswipe victim: The 3126 got pushed off the track by cab-forward Number 4130 at Fields, Oregon, on July 16, 1947. The Pacific was scrapped.
S.S. Harper photo from the collection of Kenneth G. Johnsen

Top: By the late forties and early fifties older Pacifics were not worth rebuilding. The 2401, wrecked earlier at Manteca and rebuilt, suffered another altercation in 1950 and was scrapped. Photo at Los Angeles in August 1950 by Gerald M. Best, from the collection of Arnold S. Menke.

Above right: After its Selma wreck, the 2479 was taken to Sacramento where it was rebuilt and then put in nearly 20 more years of service. It is still with us today, having been placed on display at the Santa Clara County Fairgrounds in San Jose. *James E. Boynton photo*

Sport model heavy 0-6-2 switcher with a roomy, fair-weather cab? Well, not quite. Pacific 2422 on Train 53 hit a truck at Fresno in 1937. The "Sacto" shops performed a complete rebuild. *Robert B. McNeel collection*

Above left: Pacific 2451 and Mountain 4355 were double-heading on Train 76 when they hit a gravel truck at Glendale, California, on October 16, 1936. The 4-8-2 is being righted while the Pacific waits its turn in the dirt.
Gerald M. Best photo from Robert B. McNeel collection

Top: The 2451's tender came completely off its frame in the Glendale accident. *Gerald M. Best photo from the collection of Arnold S. Menke*

Left and above right: Not exactly wrecked, but utterly helpless just the same, Number 2480 broke a side rod in 1938 and had to be towed to the shops.
Kenneth Frick photo from Ted Wurm collection

Above: Beginning of the end: the first Pacific to be scrapped was Number 2421 at West Oakland in May of 1939. By late 1959 only three of the 146-unit fleet remained.
Milliard Brown photo from the collection of Harre Demoro

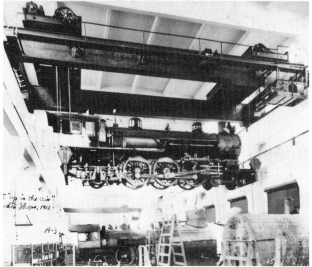

Hoists with cables strong enough to lift entire locomotives enabled the larger shops, such as Houston, to perform major rebuilds of wrecked engines, not to mention construction of all-new locomotives.　　　　*Collection of Arnold S. Menke*

The din of escaping steam, the clank of the side rods, the whine of the turbogenerator, punctuated by occasional blasts on a melodic, multi-chimed whistle made the S.P. Pacifics seem lifelike. *Mac Gaddis photo*

Strictly Personal

EVERYONE WHO WAS fortunate enough to have lived in the days of Southern Pacific steam operation has certain memories of sights, smells and sounds which sometimes, by the mere mention of the name of a town or place on the railroad, come back vividly into mind.

Hearing names like Burlingame, Palo Alto, and San Jose can conjure the image of a big silver-faced but otherwise black steam engine, its headlight shining at you from a point pleasingly below center on the smokebox door. The engine appears to be anxious to be on its way. Thinly transparent black smoke rises from a generously large smokestack perched above an almost bald forehead.

Steam emanates from someplace else further back on the boiler. And what a boiler! No straight tube that looked like it had been on a diet, but rather as full and esthetically pleasing a contoured ("wagon top") boiler as you could place on an engine without its looking "fat." From the large forward sand dome it rises and crests just above the last tall driver, tapering just enough down to the cab to let the cab stand out and hold its rightful place of importance.

How high the cab is. A kid standing on the ground has to crane his neck to look up and wonder what manner of god lives way up in there. The engine, with its silver face and exciting sounds, seems to be a living creature. The men in the cab aren't like drivers in the sense of an automobile or truck. They appear more like little beings holding the reins while perched on the back of some huge dragon. The fire in this dragon's belly, the hissing steam, its great *mass,* leave no doubt of the tremendous power it possesses. One false move by those mortals up in the cab and it is obvious much fury would break loose.

At departure time the large black engine with the big white numbers on its cab and the words "Southern Pacific" looking very important on its tender shows how much of a living animal it really is. A melodic husky-voiced multichime whistle shouts its first words clear across town. The bell starts dinging a pointed solid ring. And as the throttle is opened and the brake released, the stack talk begins.

Bark! . . . . Bark! . . . Bark! . . Bark! . Bark! What a loud voice this creature has, each bark coming quicker than the last as it picks up speed. The smoke is erupting much more furiously now. All eyes watch the black beast, transfixed by the sounds and action even as it rounds the curve out of sight and the cars of its train clatter across the rail joints in passing.

This steam engine was unmistakably Southern Pacific. From the homemade corrugated pilot to the massive cylindrical Vanderbilt tender on six-wheel trucks, the locomotive made Southern Pacific steam a cherished memory of the glory days of railroading.

Perhaps this engine was the 2467 or the 2472 or the 2479. Regardless of which number, the Southern Pacific's heavy 4-6-2s were an esthetic high point in locomotive development. They carried with them a presence that defined steam locomotion in the West. Their never-to-be-forgotten personality quickens the pulse of one who views them even at silent rest in a park.

It is interesting to note that while function preceded form, the newer Pacifics on S.P. almost magically achieved the right balance of proportions to make an overwhelmingly captivating appearance. To say that these engines were just good-looking is an understatement.

What makes this harmony of form elements even more noteworthy is the impression one gets when looking at efforts to streamline these engines. With streamlining there was an actual attempt to make them "look good." And yet even those among us who fervently admire streamlined steam could arguably make a case for superior appearance of, say, the unadorned P-10 2479 over the San Joaquin's three streamlined P-10s. The shrouding and skyline casings look like what they were: an afterthought. The true beauty of 2484–2486 comes from the harmonious, distinctly Southern Pacific proportions of the P-10s which show through despite the shroud.

The T&NO *Sunbeams* similarly were handsome engines, but the good lines arose more from the taper of the boiler courses, the size, shape, and height off the ground of the "sport" cab, and the Vanderbilt tender than from the funnel nose or side skirt.

Probably the high point in esthetic functional design was achieved in the P-9 and P-13 classes on the T&NO. These included the last Pacifics built for the Southern Pacific. The massive semi-Vanderbilt tenders applied to these engines gave them a powerful, big league, no-nonsense appearance.

The Pacifics had their lighter moments too. They played dress-up for the movies in Hollywood, and wore patriotic red, white and blue bunting to promote War Bonds. They were the kind of engine that was always there, filling the various needs of the railroad. You took them for granted and were not surprised to see them in many kinds of service.

Pacifics worked right alongside newer, heavier power to the end of steam on S.P. The last official run of a 4-6-2 on the Southern Pacific was an excursion chartered by the

Central Coast Railway Club on January 1, 1958. Number 2475, spruced up with white tires and trim, pulled the excursionists from Niles over Altamont Pass to Tracy and back. When its fire was killed, the curtain came down on Southern Pacific 4-6-2 operation indeed as it had on all other classes of S.P. steam locomotives. More than three decades would pass before an S.P. Pacific would operate again.

Top: S.P.'s capable Pacifics were called on to fill various roles over the years, and did so with ease. Flags, bunting, and special decoration for the Third Liberty Loan Special train illustrates just one such occasion. Engine is Number 2460, one of two Sacramento-built Pacifics, shown at Oakland, California, in 1909. *Norman Holmes collection via James E. Boynton*

Above: The author's favorite Pacific picture, snapped by Will Whittaker on the final 4-6-2 run in January 1958, shows off the clean lines and handsome proportions of the S.P. Pacifics. The 2475 is having its last hurrah in Niles Canyon, California.

Opposite top: Neither @#!* nor high water seems to be able to stop the 2409 as it prances through flooded Stege, California, in February of 1940. *Arnold S. Menke collection*

Opposite below: Whether beating the Keystone Cops to a crossing in an old silent movie or masquerading as an elephant-eared European locomotive for a World War II flick, Southern Pacific's 4-6-2s were seen in a variety of motion pictures over the years. Photo is at Los Angeles in November 1947.
Gerald M. Best photo
from the collection of James E. Boynton

Opposite below: "A silver faced engine . . . anxious to be on its way . . . thinly transparent black smoke rising from its stack . . ." the 2469 on Train 248, the *El Dorado,* was captured in the twilight of its years at Martinez, California, in this pleasing photo by Robert A. Campbell, Sr.

Opposite top: If we agree that Southern Pacific rostered the most handsome Pacifics in the land, then what is this homely thing doing on the turntable at Santa Barbara, California? And besides, who ever heard of an S.P. 4-6-2 in the 2900 series? During World War II Southern Pacific experienced a motive power shortage and leased locomotives from other railroads. One such engine was this Burlington 4-6-2 which made its home at Santa Barbara long enough to acquire the standard S.P. hoods over headlight and classification lamps.

Photo by Robert B. McNeel

Above: High mounted cab, wagon top boiler, below center headlight, corrugated pilot, husky Vanderbilt tender on six-wheel trucks: all these were elements that helped create the distinct beauty of S.P. Pacifics.

Photo by Mac Gaddis in October 1953

Above: The smooth uncluttered boiler jacket of 2466 glistens in the afternoon sun. Tenders belonging to the Pacifics' successors, the Mountains and Northerns, share roundhouse garden tracks with the husky 4-6-2. This photo by Mac Gaddis captures a bit of the feeling of what it was like to be around the engine terminals in the days of steam.

Left: No nonsense. That was the look achieved by T&NO's handsome Pacifics of the P-9 and P-13 classes. The huge semi-Vanderbilt tenders they pulled were usually reserved for heavier engines. Photo at San Antonio, Texas, on September 20, 1937, from the collection of James E. Boynton.

The Survivors

DURING THE DECADE of the 1950s, American steam locomotion on major railroads ended. Southern Pacific, like most other railroads, was aware of the radical technological change coming with dieselization and offered to give steam locomotives to various communities along its lines so that specimens of the "iron horse" could be preserved.

Towns along the line were informed that they should provide a final resting place and make a formal request in order to get a locomotive. Suitable final resting places were most often found in city parks or at fairgrounds. Typically a local service organization would donate funds and labor to get the locomotive moved from S.P. tracks to its display site.

Three of S.P.'s Pacifics thus escaped scrap and were preserved in cities around the San Francisco Bay. P-10 Number 2479 was donated to the Santa Clara County Fairgrounds at San Jose on September 6, 1958.

P-8 Number 2472 was donated to San Mateo County Fairgrounds at San Mateo on April 10, 1959. Another P-8, Number 2467, was donated to the city of Oakland on July 25, 1960, being placed on display in Harrison Square Railroad Park along with a pair of passenger cars.

Deterioration from the elements and indignities wrought by vandals have not hidden the clean lines and beautiful proportions of these machines from those who appreciate such things.

Mike Mangini and a few other enthusiasts who had done volunteer work on the American Freedom Train in the mid-1970s admired the 2472 reposing at San Mateo and asked themselves, "Why not?" They had seen what money, hard work, money, dedication, money, expertise, and more money could do with the Freedom Train and its locomotives.

The 2472 was a handsome and powerful engine. The population of railfans as well as non-railfan potential riders was dense enough in the Bay Area that one could reasonably expect steam-powered excursions to be successful. The group obtained San Mateo County's blessing and Project 2472, Inc. was born.

The restoration of 2472 caught nationwide attention and attracted volunteers like a magnet. Along with refurbishment of the locomotive and tender, the group acquired a fleet of passenger cars to make up its train.

Pacific fever was contagious. Project 2467 sprang up with the announced intention to restore the P-8 in Oak-

The Pacifics were always showing up on short-haul trains in the years after they were bumped from the flagships by larger power. The 2467 is on the westbound *Sacramento Daylight* at Lathrop, California, not long before the engine's retirement in 1956.
*Photo by Al Augenstein
from the collection of Tom Gray*

Above: Southern Pacific P-8 2467 was placed on display in Harrison Square Railroad Park in Oakland, California, in 1960. Shorn of its "collectible" hardware, the engine was still a handsome piece of machinery when this photo was taken 26 years later. *Photo by Kenneth G. Johnsen*

Top: In May of 1940, Oakland's future Pacific was hauling freight on the Surf Local out of Santa Barbara. Boiler tube pilot had not yet been replaced by one of corrugated steel.
Robert B. McNeel photo

land for operation on the Napa Valley Wine Train. 2467 volunteers and 2472 volunteers agreed to share information, expertise, and tools for the mutual benefit of each.

Not to be outdone, enthusiasts in San Jose began tackling a similar restoration of P-10 Number 2479 at the fairgrounds there. The steam drought that began in 1957 when S.P. was killing the last fires, seems to be showing signs of abatement now.

The earlier, straight-boilered Pacifics did not fare so well, most of them meeting their demise by 1950 or so. However, thanks to a historical event near the beginning of the Twentieth Century, we can today touch a virtual P-1 clone.

The Southern Pacific and Union Pacific fell under the singular control of Edward H. Harriman in 1901. Under Harriman, a set of Common Standards was adopted in 1904. Locomotives were ordered in large batches from the builders and were parceled out to S.P. and U.P. as the need arose.

An order to Schenectady for Pacifics in 1904 was thus divided between the two railroads. The S.P. engines are now long gone, but one of the Union Pacific engines, Number 3206, survived and is today undergoing restoration at Spokane Interstate Fairgrounds.

The close similarities between this engine and an S.P. P-1 or P-3 are striking, especially when one considers the fact that the 3206's modern-day appearance evolved in a separate environment from S.P.'s Pacifics. Thank you, Mr. Harriman.

Opposite top: Had the fatal 1937 accident (see Chapter 4) of 2479 at Selma, California, occurred later in the Pacific's career, this engine might have been scrapped. The 4-6-2 was rebuilt, however, and gave nearly 20 more years of service. Today it reposes at San Jose, the wild adventure of half a century ago nearly forgotten. *Arnold S. Menke collection*

Opposite below: Spunky four-year-old. When this picture of 2479 at San Luis Obispo was taken in June of 1927, Pacifics were the pride of the fleet. The care and attention accorded these engines can be seen in the high polish and neatly applied striping.
Photo by Tom Taber from the collection of Arnold S. Menke

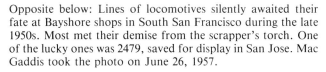

Opposite below: Lines of locomotives silently awaited their fate at Bayshore shops in South San Francisco during the late 1950s. Most met their demise from the scrapper's torch. One of the lucky ones was 2479, saved for display in San Jose. Mac Gaddis took the photo on June 26, 1957.

Opposite top: Good-looking 2479, seen here with smaller tender and boiler tube pilot, is leaving Oakland's 16th Street station in 1939.   *James E. Boynton collection*

Above: Resting in a pleasant, tree-lined corner of the Santa Clara County Fairgrounds in San Jose, California, the 2479 can only ponder what the future might hold in store. Photo by Kenneth G. Johnsen on October 25, 1986.

Above: Right and left side views of what was destined to become the best-known of Southern Pacific's 4-6-2 locomotives. View of the right side at Sacramento in February of 1937 shows 2472's older style headlight, boiler tube pilot, and smaller "Southern Pacific Lines" lettering on tender. James E. Boynton took the photo. Fireman's side view at Mission Bay in November of 1949 shows the locomotive as it looked in its last ten years or so of operation.

R. Berry photo from the collection of Arnold S. Menke

Left: Near Martinez, California, along the shore of San Pablo Bay, the 2472 hustles with No. 229, the westbound *Governor,* on November 20, 1941.   *Robert E. Searle photo from the collection of James E. Boynton*

Above: The 2472 and a train of Harriman coaches: this is how Project 2472 members envision their engine and train when their project reaches fruition.

Will Whittaker photo from Arnold S. Menke collection

Opposite top right: John Teshara prepares the smokebox front for its lid on October 26, 1986. The 2472 passed its hydro test to 265 pounds with flying colors, keeping pressure as high as 210 pounds a half hour later.   *Kenneth G. Johnsen photo*

Opposite center right: Instead of moving the 2472 to some abandoned factory building or borrowing space in an engine-house, Project 2472 volunteers elected to perform the rebuild at the engine's display site on the San Mateo County Fair-grounds. A work area was fenced off and a container van was brought in to serve as a tool and parts shed.

Kenneth G. Johnsen photo

Top left: Pilot truck frame required major rebuilding. Jacks were used to lift the engine off its wheels and blocks supporting a beam at each end kept it in the air.
Kenneth G. Johnsen photo in February of 1987

Left: A peek into 2472's firebox. The locomotive was reflued in the enviably short time of three days. Steve Maffuci and crew replaced 123 staybolts. *Kenneth G. Johnsen photo*

Above: This splendid pan shot of 2472 shows what the Pacifics did on weekends when they were not involved in commute service. The future steam star is seen in June of 1955 pulling a string of 25 or 30 cars of strawberries from the Salinas Valley to San Jose. Neil Vodden took the photo from a pacing car near Gilroy. *Peter Kunedt collection*

Opposite top and bottom: Thanks to the 1904 Harriman Common Standards for Southern Pacific and Union Pacific locomotives, we can today lay our hands on a P-1 clone. Union Pacific 3206 (above) was built along with the first five S.P. Pacifics at Schenectady in 1904. The Union Pacific engine survived, and is today undergoing restoration by the Inland Empire Chapter of the NRHS in Spokane, Washington. *Photo at Spokane Interstate Fairgrounds by Kenneth G. Johnsen* S.P. 2431 (below) at San Francisco in 1938 provides an interesting comparison. The appearance of this P-3 is so similar to that of the 3206 that one gets the impression that, from a mechanical standpoint, the 3206 has been frozen in time since the mid-1930s. *Kenneth G. Johnsen collection*

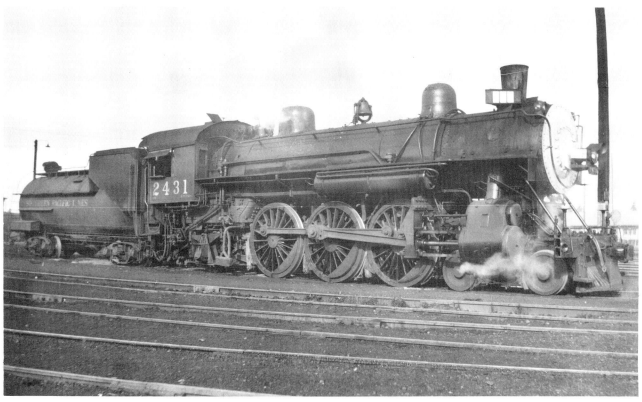

Appendix

Streamlined Pacifics

2455 (650)	Streamlining applied*	July 23, 1937 at Houston
2456 (651)	Streamlining applied	August 7, 1937 at Houston
2457 (652)	Streamlining applied	August 18, 1937 at Houston
2481	Skyline casing applied	January 27, 1948 at Bayshore
2482	Skyling casing applied	August 30, 1947 at Bayshore
2483	Skyline casing applied	July 29, 1940 at Bayshore
2484	Streamlining applied**	May 31, 1941 at Los Angeles
	Skirting removed	April 28, 1950 at West Oakland
2485	Streamlining applied	June 20, 1941 at Los Angeles
	Skirting removed	
2486	Streamlining applied	October 14, 1941 at Los Angeles
	Skirting removed	April 26, 1950 at West Oakland
2487	Skyline casing applied	August 18, 1947 at Bayshore
2488	Skyline casing applied	January 6, 1941 at Bayshore
2489	Skyline casing applied	March 13, 1940 at Los Angeles
2491	Skyline casing applied	August 25, 1939 at Los Angeles

*Streamlining on Numbers **2455, 2456,** and **2457** included skyline casing, running-board skirting, streamlined pilot, bullet nose, "sport" cab, and Daylight paint scheme.

Streamlining on Numbers **2484, 2485, and **2486** included skyline casing, runningboard skirting, "sport" cab, and Daylight paint scheme.

Classification by Equipment

	Class	Superheater	Feedwater Heater	Booster
Pacific Lines				
	P-1	X		
	P-1a	X	X	
	P-1b	X		X
	P-1c	X	X	X
	P-3	X		
	P-4	X	X	X
	P-5	X		
	P-6	X		
	P-6a	X	X	
	P-7	X		
	P-8	X	X	
	P-8a	X	X	X
	P-10	X	X	
	P-10a	X	X	X
	P-11	X		
	P-12	X	X	
Atlantic Lines				
	P-5	X	X	X
	P-6	X	X	X
	P-9	X	X	X
	P-13	X	X	X
	P-14	X	X	X

Class P-1, Schenectady, 1904.   *Alco Historic Photos*

Original Tenders for SP 4-6-2s

Compiled by Arnold Menke

Locomotive	Original Tender	Original Fuel
P-1: 2400-2404	7000 Vanderbilt	coal

Schenectady 1904

Note: These tenders came with arch bar trucks.

P-1: 2405-2419	9000 rectangular	coal and oil (see note)

Baldwin 1906

Note: 2405-2410, 2417-2419 were built as coal burners ; 2411-2416 were built as oil burners. These were the first Pacific Tenders equipped with vestibules. Trucks were arch bar type. These tenders became part of class SP 90-R-1 in 1922.

P-1: 2420-2421	7000 Vanderbilt	coal

Baldwin 1907

Note: Equipped with vestibule. Arch bar trucks.

P-1: 2422-2427	9000 rectangular	oil

Baldwin 1907

Note: Equipped with vestibule. Arch bar trucks. These tenders became part of class SP 90-R-1 in 1922.

P-11: 3100-3103	7000 rectangular	coal

Baldwin 1907

Built as EP&SW 140-143

Note: These tenders were EP&SW class G1, Nos. 7-10; they came with arch bar trucks. According to statements in EP&SW diagram books, these rectangular tenders were rebuilt in 1913-1914 to the SC type used behind the rest of the P-11s.

P-11: 3104-3109	7000 semicylindrical	coal

Baldwin 1907

Built as EP&SW 144-149

Note: These tenders were EP&SW class M1, Nos. 1-6. They had Andrews cast steel trucks that had a rather unusual and distinctive high arch. These tenders became part of SP class 70-SC-1 when the EP&SW was absorbed in 1924, and were no longer used with P-11s after 1929-30 with one exception (engine No. 3102).

P-3: 2428-2437	7000 Vanderbilt	oil

Baldwin 1911

Note: Equipped with vestibule. Andrews cast steel trucks. These tenders became part of class SP 70-C-3 in 1922.

P-5: 900-909	9000 Vanderbilt	oil

Baldwin 1912

Note: Equipped with vestibule. Andrews cast steel trucks. Became part of T&NO class 90-C-1 in the twenties.

P-5: 2438-2452	7000 Vanderbilt	oil

Baldwin 1912

Note: Equipped with vestibule. Andrews cast steel trucks. Grouped in SP classes 70-C-2 and 3 in 1922.

P-6: 920-931	9000 Vanderbilt	oil

Brooks 1913

Note: Equipped with vestibule. Andrews cast steel trucks. Became part of T&NO class 90-C-1 in the twenties.

P-6: 2453-2458	9000 Vanderbilt	oil

Brooks 1913

Note: Equipped with vestibule. Andrews cast steel trucks. Became part of SP class 90-C-2 in 1922.

Class P-3, S.P. Sacramento, 1917.

James E. Boynton collection

P-12: 3120-3129   9000 rectangular   coal
Brooks 1917
Built as EP&SW 160-169
Note: Equipped with vestibule and pedestal trucks. These tenders were class Y1, Nos. 1-10 on the EP&SW. They became SP class 90-R-6, Nos. 7770-7779 when acquired in 1924. Converted to oil in 1929-30.

P-7: 2476-2477   9000 Vanderbilt   oil
Lima 1917
Built as AE 701-702
Note: Equipped with vestibule and Andrews trucks. Builder photo confirms tender behind 2476. Presumably 2477 had same tender. These tenders were placed in SP class 90-C-1 when transferred from the AE in 1922.

P-3: 2459-2460   7000 Vanderbilt   oil
Southern Pacific 1917-18
Note: Both locomotives were supplied with existing tenders that still had intact vestibules and arch bar trucks. 2459 had No. 70-58 which became 70-C-3 7115 in 1922. 2460 had No. 70-63 which became 70-C-3 7116 in 1922.

Note: By 1920 buffers were systematically being removed from SP and T&NO tenders equipped with vestibules, and this activity was probably complete by the early 1920s. The vestibules themselves were often left in place for many years after the buffer had been removed.

P-8: 2461-2475   12000 Vanderbilt   oil
Baldwin 1921
Note: These tenders came with Commonwealth cast-steel frames with integral end sills. They rode on 4-wheel pedestal trucks. These tenders were originally numbered 120-1 through 15 under the 1913 tender classification, but in 1922 they became part of class 120-C-1, Nos. 8500-8014.

P-9: 622-630   12000 Vanderbilt   oil
Baldwin 1923
Note: T&NO class 120-C-1, Nos. 2400-2408. These tenders had same frame and trucks as the P-8 tenders but differed from most SP & T&NO 120-C-1s in having 36-inch-diameter wheels, instead of 33-inch.

P-10: 2478-2483   12000 Vanderbilt   oil
Baldwin 1923-24
Note: These tenders came with Commonwealth cast-steel frames with integral end sills and 4-wheel pedestal trucks with clasp brakes. They were part of SP class 120-C-2, Nos. 8644-8649.

P-10: 2484-2491   12000 Vanderbilt   oil
Baldwin 1924
Note: These tenders came with Commonwealth cast-steel frames with integral end sills and 6-wheel Commonwealth trucks. They were part of SP class 120-C-3, Nos. 8685-8692.

P-13: 631-633   16000 Vanderbilt   oil
Baldwin 1928
Note: These tenders had cast-steel water bottom frames from Commonwealth Steel and had 6-wheel Commonwealth trucks. These tenders were in T&NO class 160-C-2.

Note: In 1928-29 the T&NO either built or had built by Baldwin, extra 160-C-2s that were then applied to their P-9s.

P-14: 650-652   12000 Vanderbilt
Rebuilt T&NO 1937   (see note)
Note: 650 had 120-C-6 No. 2435 (former SP No. 8723). 651-652 had 120-C-3 Nos. 2425 and 2427 (651 had 2427, 652 had 2425). These three were originally Pacific Lines tenders, but were transferred to the T&NO with 2-10-2s (the two 120-C-3s) and 2455 (the 120-C-6). They differed from "normal" SP and T&NO 120-C-3s and 6s in a number of ways, but principally the wheels were changed from 33 inches in diameter to 36 inches, and the oil tank side was extended forward by the addition of an 8½-inch steel strip that made the tank even with the forward end of the water tank. This was strictly cosmetic; the oil tank capacity remained unchanged. Tender 2425 had trucks normally used under tenders of class 120-C-6.

Class P-5, Baldwin, 1912.
Railroad Museum of Pennsylvania collection

2472 LOCOMOTIVE TENDER ASSIGNMENTS

Form 7070   C.S. 1-28-7880-8

ASSIGNED		ASSIGNED		ASSIGNED		ASSIGNED		ASSIGNED		ASSIGNED	
TENDER NO.	DATE	TENDER NO.	DATE	TENDER NO.	DATE	TENDER NO.	DATE	TENDER NO.	DATE	TENDER NO.	DATE
851v	8-29-24	8700	4-4-37	8678	4-30-44			120-C-1		120-C-5	120-C-3
8503	2-27-25	8721	4-19-37	8666	7-5-44	120 - C-3				120-C-6	"
851v	3-2-25	Shop Oak	4-22-37								
8508	7-29-25	8700	6-11-37		Vac. Adv. Auth. JAN 18 1957	San Jose					
8512	9-25-25	Sh. Oak	1-6-38							120-C-3	
8508	10-31-25	8693	1-8-38								
8512	12-21-25	Sh Oak	3-15-38							120-C-6	
Shop Og	3-30-37	8717	3-29-38							120-C-8	
8512	4-9-27	8767	4-18-38					120-C-3		120-C-3	
8678	5-26-27	8654	8-30-38					120-C-1		120-C-8	
8512	6-5-27	8767	9-13-38								
Shop Og	1-4-28	Unasgd oak	5-20-39					"		120-C-6	
8512	1-31-28	8769	5-22-39					120-C-5		"	
8700	1-25-29	8711	1-20-40							120-C-3	
Sh. SL	2-5-29	8658	11-26-40			15				"	
4152	5-?-29	8678	7-7-41					"		"	
8700	7-9-29	8684	3-10-44							"	
Spare	3-14-34	8678	3-20-44					"		120-C-5	
8700	4-23-34	Ua oak	4-13-44					120-C-3			
8693	9-3-35	8708	4-18-44					120-C-5		120-C-3	
8700	9-1-35	8678	4-21-44								
Sh Oak	4-2-37	Ua oak	4-24-44								

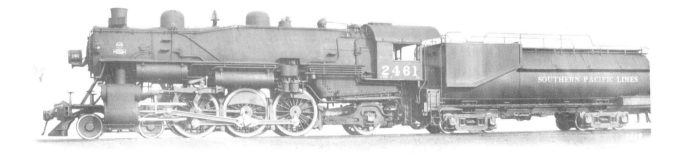

Class P-8, Baldwin, 1921.
Railroad Museum of Pennsylvania collection

12473

LOCOMOTIVE TENDER ASSIGNMENTS

Form 7070 — C.S. 1-46-7500-S

ASSIGNED		ASSIGNED		ASSIGNED		ASSIGNED		ASSIGNED		ASSIGNED	
TENDER NO.	DATE	TENDER NO.	DATE	TENDER NO.	DATE	TENDER NO.	DATE	TENDER NO.	DATE	TENDER NO.	DATE
8513	5-6-22	Shop Oak	9-30-32	8668	6-30-44			120-C-1			120-C-3
8502	7-3-25	8693	10-10-32	Ship	4-3-47					120-C-3	
8513	8-5-25	Spare Oak	2-7-34	8721	4-26-47						120-C-6
Shop	?-??-25	8693	3-13-34	8765	5-29-53					"	120-C-8
8513	9-30-25	Sh Oak	9-3-35	8660	11-19-55						120-C-3
Shop	??-25	8693	9-19-35							"	
Spare Oak	1-?3-?7	8719	1-26-37			(15)				120-C-6	
8693	?-10-?7	8684	3-15-37					120-C-3		120-C-3	
8512	3-30-27	8693	3-26-37					120-C-1		"	
8693	4-14-27	Sh Oak	4-22-37					120-C-3			
8678	9-13-27	8644	5-22-37							"	
8693	11-9-27	8693	6-11-37			Vac. Adv. Auth.	SEP 19 1955 "Oakland"				
Shop	3-22-28	8700	1-8-38							120-C-5	
8678	4-12-28	Spare Oak	10-12-38					"			
8693	5-5-28	8714	10-13-38					"		120-C-6	
8507	11-9-28	8769	10-14-38					120-C-1		"	
8502	1-4-29	8700	11-17-38					"		120-C-5	
8693	2-28-29	8749	8-16-39					120-C-3		120-C-8	
Shop Oak	5-1-30	Shop Oak	2-14-41								
8693	7-24-30	8684	3-14-41					"		120-C-3	
Shop Oak	9-30-32	Shop RH	1-31-42					"			
8693	10-10-32	8660	2-5-44					"		"	

Class P-7, Lima, 1922. *Arnold S. Menke collection*

Pacific Lines

Engine Number	Class	Builder	Serial Number	In-Service Date	Vacated Date	Notes
2400	P-1c	Schenectady	30000	9-04	11-8-48	Scr. Bayshore 10-8-48
2401	P-4	Schenectady	30001	9-04	9-20-50	Scr. Los Angeles 10-14-50
2402	P-4	Schenectady	30002	9-04	3-31-53	Scr. Bayshore 5-21-53
2403	P-1b	Schenectady	30003	9-04	7-26-51	S/Scr. Tracy 8-21-51, Scr. Luria 11-14-51
2404	P-1b	Schenectady	30004	9-04		Sold S.P. de Mex. 12-21-51, Re# 300. Returned 12-21-52, Scr. El Paso 1-23-53
2405	P-1c	Baldwin	27366	3-6-06	7-26-51	S/Scr. Tracy 9-28-51, Scr. Luria 11-15-51
2406	P-1c	Baldwin	27367	3-6-06	7-26-51	Vac. Tracy, Scr. Hyman-Michaels 10-1-51
2407	P-1c	Baldwin	27368	3-8-06	6-26-52	Vac. W. Oakland, Scr. Sacramento 9-21-52
2408	P-1a	Baldwin	27369	3-8-06		Sold S.P. de Mex. 12-21-51, Re# 301. Returned 7-22-53, Scr. El Paso 8-53
2409	P-4	Baldwin	27465	3-15-06	10-17-51	Vac. Bayshore, Scr. Hyman-Michaels 1-3-52
2410	P-4	Baldwin	27466	3-16-06	4-20-54	Vac. Oakland, S/Scr. Purdy 9-8-54
2411	P-1	Baldwin	28660	9-17-06	4-20-54	Vac. Oakland, S/Scr. Purdy 9-8-54
2412	P-1	Baldwin	28673	9-15-06	6-13-51	Leased S.P. de Mex. 7-9-48 to 1-22-51. Scr. Tucson 7-23-51
2413	P-1	Baldwin	28674	9-24-06	12-26-47	Scr. Sacramento 1-21-48
2414	P-4	Baldwin	28714	9-22-06	10-6-54	Scr. Bayshore 12-22-54
2415	P-1b	Baldwin	28737	10-5-06	7-26-51	Vac. Tracy, Scr. Luria 10-30-51
2416	P-1	Baldwin	28738	10-8-06	4-28-47	Vac. Bakersfield, Scr. Los Angeles 4-14-47
2417	P-1	Baldwin	28826	9-27-06	7-26-51	Leased S.P. de Mex. 7-15-48 to 5-24-51. Vac. Tucson, S/Scr. National Metals 8-31-51
2418	P-1	Baldwin	28797	11-2-06	11-8-48	Scr. Bayshore 10-12-48
2419	P-4	Baldwin	28867	10-31-06	10-3-51	Vac. Tucson, S/Scr. National Metals 10-23-51
2420	P-4	Baldwin	30762	6-23-07	7-26-51	Vac. Oakland, Scr. Purdy 11-2-51
2421	P-1a	Baldwin	30763	6-23-07	1-1-34	Scr. Oakland 5-4-39 (First one scrapped)
2422	P-4	Baldwin	30785	6-30-07	7-26-51	Vac. Oakland, Scr. Purdy 11-16-51
2423	P-1	Baldwin	30786	6-30-07	12-17-48	Scr. Los Angeles 1-10-49
2424	P-4	Baldwin	30827	7-12-07	7-26-51	Vac. Los Angeles, S/Scr. Hyman-Michaels 8-31-51
2425	P-1	Baldwin	30706	7-13-07	1-27-49	Scr. Bayshore 2-9-49
2426	P-1	Baldwin	30923	7-25-07	11-28-49	Vac. Eugene, Scr. Brooklyn 12-22-49
2427	P-1	Baldwin	30924	7-27-07	2-24-49	Scr. Los Angeles 3-14-49
2428	P-3	Baldwin	36058	3-25-11	12-26-52	Sold S.P. de Mex. 12-21-51, Re# 302. Returned 12-21-52, Scr. El Paso 2-17-53
2429	P-3	Baldwin	36059	3-29-11	7-28-47	Scr. Los Angeles 7-5-47
2430	P-3	Baldwin	36060	3-31-11	2-24-47	Scr. Los Angeles 3-29-47
2431	P-3	Baldwin	36061	3-31-11	4-20-54	Vac. Oakland, S/Scr. Purdy 9-8-54
2432	P-3	Baldwin	36062	4-1-11	6-26-52	Vac. Oakland, Scr. Sacramento 9-5-52
2433	P-3	Baldwin	36063	4-7-11	9-1-52	Sold S.P. de Mex. 12-21-51, Re# 303, Scr. 5-53
2434	P-3	Baldwin	36064	4-8-11	9-15-47	Scr. El Paso 9-20-47
2435	P-3	Baldwin	36065	4-5-11	5-10-48	Scr. Bayshore 3-16-48
2436	P-4	Baldwin	36066	4-12-11	4-10-52	Scr. Bayshore 6-5-52
2437	P-3	Baldwin	36067	4-14-11	8-17-49	Vac. Eugene, Scr. Brooklyn 11-29-49
2438	P-5	Baldwin	36168	9-30-12	2-24-49	Scr. Bayshore 3-14-49
2439	P-5	Baldwin	38169	10-4-12		Sold S.P. de Mex. 12-21-51, Re# 304, Scr. 2-56
2440	P-5	Baldwin	38192	10-3-12	12-14-50	Scr. Sacramento 1-24-51
2441	P-5	Baldwin	38193	10-7-12		Sold S.P. de Mex. 12-21-51, Re# 305, Returned 12-21-52, Scr. El Paso 1-16-53
2442	P-5	Baldwin	38194	10-13-12	7-29-47	Scr. Los Angeles 7-23-47
2443	P-5	Baldwin	38195	10-14-12	3-31-53	Scr. Oakland 5-11-53
2444	P-5	Baldwin	38196	10-8-12	7-26-51	Vac. Tucson, S/Scr. Eastern Iron & Metals 8-21-51
2445	P-5	Baldwin	38137	9-28-12	12-28-49	Wrecked on S.P. de Mex., Scr. 2-9-50
2446	P-5	Baldwin	38138	9-29-12	7-29-47	Scr. Los Angeles 7-30-47
2447	P-5	Baldwin	38139	9-30-12	4-10-52	Scr. Los Angeles 5-15-52
2448	P-5	Baldwin	38140	9-22-12		Sold S.P. de Mex. 12-21-51, Re# 306, Scr. 3-53
2449	P-5	Baldwin	38141	9-22-12	10-21-52	Scr. Sacramento 12-12-52
2450	P-5	Baldwin	38142	9-28-12	10-3-51	Vac. Tucson, S/Scr. National Metals 10-23-51
2451	P-5	Baldwin	38143	9-30-12	12-14-50	Vac. Oakland, Scr. Sacramento 1-12-51
2452	P-5	Baldwin	38144	10-3-12		Sold S.P. de Mex. 12-21-51, Re# 307, Scr. 7-53
2453	P-6	American	53333	8-12-13	9-19-55	Scr. Bayshore 11-2-55
2454	P-6a	American	53334	8-3-13	10-2-57	Vac. Bayshore, Scr. Purdy 8-10-59

Above: Class P-13, Baldwin, 1928. Note lighter colored boiler jacket and additional striping.

Railroad Museum of Pennsylvania collection

Top: All of the P-10 class from Numbers 2481 through 2491 received skyline casings except the 2490, seen here at Dunsmuir helping a GS-6 with train No. 20, the *Klamath*.

Guy L. Dunscomb photo on August 28, 1948, from the collection of James E. Boynton

Engine Number	Class	Builder	Serial Number	In-Service Date	Vacated Date	Notes
2455	P-6	American	53335	8-4-13		Leased T&NO 2-5-37, Re# 650 7-23-37, Sold T&NO 5-31-46, S/Scr. Houston Compressed Steel 3-25-54
2456	P-6a	American	53336	8-5-13		Leased T&NO 2-6-37, Re# 651 8-7-37, Sold T&NO 5-31-46, S/Scr. Houston Compressed Steel 3-25-54
2457	P-6	American	53337	8-9-13		Leased T&NO 2-27-37, Re# 652 8-18-37, Sold T&NO 5-31-46, Scr. Houston 12-2-53
2458	P-6	American	53338	8-12-13	11-15-55	Vac. Bayshore, S/Scr. Purdy 2-18-57
2459	P-3	S.P. Sacto	76	9-20-17	3-20-52	Vac. Los Angeles, S/Scr. Luria 3-31-52
2460	P-3	S.P. Sacto	84	4-18-18	12-11-48	Scr. Bayshore 12-30-48
2461	P-8	Baldwin	54396	3-5-21	5-25-55	Vac. Oakland, S/Scr. California Metals 7-1-55
2462	P-8	Baldwin	54397	3-4-21	10-6-54	Vac. Bayshore, Scr. Purdy 11-13-54
2463	P-8	Baldwin	54468	3-7-21	6-12-56	Vac. Oakland, Scr. Luria 2-27-57
2464	P-8	Baldwin	54469	3-8-21	11-23-53	Scr. Bayshore 1-18-54
2465	P-8	Baldwin	54470	3-18-21	5-14-56	Vac. Bayshore, Scr. Purdy 6-15-56
2466	P-8	Baldwin	54471	3-18-21	12-26-56	Vac. Oakland, Scr. Luria 2-9-57
2467	P-8	Baldwin	54472	3-24-21	12-26-56	Vac. Oakland, Donated to City of Oakland 7-25-60
2468	P-8	Baldwin	54473	3-25-21	5-14-56	Vac. Bayshore, Scr. Purdy 6-12-56
2469	P-8	Baldwin	54474	4-4-21	2-8-55	Vac. Oakland, S/Scr. Luria 4-13-55
2470	P-8	Baldwin	54475	4-3-21	9-9-53	Scr. Bayshore 10-12-53
2471	P-8	Baldwin	54476	4-13-21	9-9-57	Vac. Oakland, Scr. California Metals 4-9-59
2472	P-8	Baldwin	54477	4-15-21	2-7-57	Vac. San Jose, Donated to San Mateo County 4-10-59
2473	P-8	Baldwin	54478	4-18-21	9-19-55	Vac. Oakland, S/Scr. Luria 12-20-55
2474	P-8	Baldwin	54479	4-27-21	3-31-53	Scr. Bayshore 5-15-53
2475	P-8a	Baldwin	54480	5-11-21	5-21-58	Vac. Oakland, S/Scr. California Metals 3-25-59
2476	P-7	Lima	5424	2-17-22	9-24-58	Blt. 1917 as Arizona Eastern 701, Vac. Bayshore, S/Scr. National Metals 7-14-59
2477	P-7	Lima	5425	3-31-22	9-24-58	Blt. 1917 as Arizona Eastern 702, Vac. Bayshore, S/Scr. National Metals 7-14-59
2478	P-10	Baldwin	57227	12-1-23	1-14-54	Vac. Bayshore, Scr. Sacramento 4-13-54
2479	P-10	Baldwin	57228	12-1-23	6-12-56	Vac. Bayshore, Donated to Santa Clara County 9-6-58
2480	P-10	Baldwin	57254	12-21-23	4-20-54	Vac. Bayshore, Scr. Purdy 7-28-54
2481	P-10	Baldwin	57255	12-22-23	1-14-54	Scr. Bayshore 3-8-54
2482	P-10	Baldwin	57264	12-27-23	3-14-56	Vac. Bayshore, S/Scr. California Metals 7-5-56
2483	P-10	Baldwin	57366	12-26-23	9-2-54	Vac. Oakland, Scr. Sacramento 11-19-54
2484	P-10a	Baldwin	57630	4-9-24	5-21-58	Vac. Oakland, S/Scr. National Metals 5-7-59

Engine Number	Class	Builder	Serial Number	In-Service Date	Vacated Date	Notes
2485	P-10a	Baldwin	57631	4-10-24	11-24-54	Scr. Sacramento 8-29-55
2486	P-10a	Baldwin	57632	4-12-24	2-8-56	Scr. Bayshore 3-28-56
2487	P-10a	Baldwin	57633	12-12-24	11-29-57	Vac. Bayshore, S/Scr. National Metals 7-14-59
2488	P-10a	Baldwin	57634	12-12-24	7-22-55	Vac. Oakland, S/Scr. Luria 10-17-55
2489	P-10a	Baldwin	57652	12-12-24	1-18-57	Vac. Bayshore, S/Scr. Purdy 2-8-57
2490	P-10a	Baldwin	57653	12-18-24	9-19-55	Vac. Oakland, Scr. Sacramento 1-13-56
2491	P-10a	Baldwin	57654		9-27-56	Vac. Bayshore, Scr. Purdy 11-26-56
3100	P-11	Baldwin	32437	12-07	12-14-49	Leased NWP 7-28-38, Returned 5-13-41, Scr. Brooklyn 1-23-50 (EP&SW 140)
3101	P-11	Baldwin	32446	12-07	7-28-47	Leased NWP 6-18-38, Returned 5-7-41, Scr. Los Angeles 3-12-48 (EP&SW 141)
3102	P-11	Baldwin	32447	12-07	10-7-48	Leased NWP 6-18-38, Returned 5-14-41, Scr. Sacramento 11-15-48 (EP&SW 142)
3103	P-11	Baldwin	32448	12-07	1-31-39	Scr. Bayshore 3-25-39 (EP&SW 143)
3104	P-11	Baldwin	32470	12-07	9-20-50	Leased NWP 6-17-38, Returned 5-19-50, Scr. Tucson 11-30-50 (EP&SW 144)
3105	P-11	Baldwin	32471	12-07	7-1-40	Leased NWP 7-30-38, Scr. Tiburon 9-10-40 (EP&SW 145)
3106	P-11	Baldwin	32472	12-07	10-20-47	Leased NWP 6-20-38, Returned 11-15-41, Scr. Los Angeles 9-19-47 (EP&SW 146)
3107	P-11	Baldwin	32473	12-07	1-31-39	Leased NWP 6-19-38, Scr. Bayshore 3-25-39 (EP&SW 147)
3108	P-11	Baldwin	32526	12-07	11-24-48	Leased NWP 6-19-38, Returned 5-28-42, Scr. Brooklyn 12-28-48 (EP&SW 148)
3109	P-11	Baldwin	32502	12-07	9-20-50	Leased NWP 7-30-38, Returned 6-1-41, Leased S.P. de Mex. 4-12-49, Returned 5-3-50, Scr. Tucson 11-30-50 (EP&SW 149)
3120	P-12	American	57422	5-17	8-31-51	Vac. Oakland, Scr. Luria 12-10-51 (EP&SW 160)
3121	P-12	American	57423	5-17	10-5-49	Scr. Brooklyn 11-18-49 (EP&SW 161)
3122	P-12	American	57424	5-17	11-10-53	Vac. Tracy, Scr. Sacramento 12-17-53 (EP&SW 162)
3123	P-12	American	57425	5-17	11-28-52	Vac. Oakland, Scr. Sacramento 1-27-53 (EP&SW 163)
3124	P-12	American	57426	5-17	9-21-49	Scr. Brooklyn 11-8-49 (EP&SW 164)
3125	P-12	American	57427	5-17	7-26-51	Vac. Oakland, Scr. Purdy 10-25-51 (EP&SW 165)
3126	P-12	American	57428	5-17	9-13-47	Scr. Brooklyn 10-3-47 (EP&SW 166)
3127	P-12	American	57429	5-17	4-10-52	Scr. Los Angeles 5-14-52 (EP&SW 167)
3128	P-12	American	57430	5-17	7-26-51	Vac. Oakland, Scr. Hyman-Michaels 10-9-51 (EP&SW 168)
3129	P-12	American	57431	5-17	7-26-51	Vac. Tucson, S/Scr. Luria 8-31-51 (EP&SW 169)

Class P-9, Baldwin, 1923.
Railroad Museum of Pennsylvania collection

Engine Number	Original Number	Class	Builder	Serial Number	In-Service Date	Notes
600	900	P-5	Baldwin	37959	8-12	Leased Pacific Lines 7-11-53, S/Scr. Luria 11-21-55
601	901	P-5	Baldwin	37960	8-12	S/Scr. Houston 4-1-53
602	902	P-5	Baldwin	37961	8-12	Leased Pacific Lines 6-30-53, S/Scr. Luria 11-23-55
603	903	P-5	Baldwin	37962	8-12	Scr. Houston 10-9-53
604	904	P-5	Baldwin	37963	8-12	Scr. Houston 10-12-53
605	905	P-5	Baldwin	37964	8-12	Leased Pacific Lines 6-30-53, S/Scr. Luria 11-23-55
606	906	P-5	Baldwin	37981	9-12	Leased Pacific Lines 7-11-53, S/Scr. Luria 2-6-57
607	907	P-5	Baldwin	37982	9-12	S/Scr. Algiers 6-3-52
608	908	P-5	Baldwin	37983	9-12	S/Scr. 3-9-53
609	909	P-5	Baldwin	37984	9-12	S/Scr. Houston 6-3-52
610	920	P-6	American	53321	7-13	S/Scr. Houston 6-3-52
611	921	P-6	American	53322	7-13	S/Scr. Houston 6-3-52
612	922	P-6	American	53323	7-13	S/Scr. Houston 1-16-53
613	923	P-6	American	53324	7-13	S/Scr. Houston 1-16-53
614	924	P-6	American	53325	7-13	S/Scr. Houston Compressed Steel 3-12-54
615	925	P-6	American	53326	7-13	S/Scr. Houston 1-16-53
616	926	P-6	American	53327	11-13	Probably used on UP 7-13 to 11-13, S/Scr. Houston 1-16-53
617	927	P-6	American	53328	7-13	S/Scr. Commercial Metals, Houston 5-21-54
618	928	P-6	American	53329	7-13	S/Scr. Houston 6-3-52
619	929	P-6	American	53330	7-13	S/Scr. Houston 6-3-52
620	930	P-6	American	53331	7-13	S/Scr. Houston Compressed Steel 3-12-54
621	931	P-6	American	53332	7-13	Scr. Houston 1-29-54
622		P-9	Baldwin	56319	6-23	S/Scr. Commercial Metals, Houston 11-18-54
623		P-9	Baldwin	56320	6-23	Scr. Houston 1-22-54
624		P-9	Baldwin	56321	6-23	Scr. Houston 12-18-53
625		P-9	Baldwin	56483	6-23	S/Scr. Houston Compressed Steel 3-12-54

Engine Number	Original Number	Class	Builder	Serial Number	In-Service Date	Notes
626		P-9	Baldwin	56484	6-23	S/Scr. Commercial Metals, Houston 6-15-54
627		P-9	Baldwin	56485	6-23	Scr. Houston 12-21-53
628		P-9	Baldwin	56486	6-23	Scr. Houston 12-28-53
629		P-9	Baldwin	56487	8-23	Scr. Houston 1-18-54
630		P-9	Baldwin	56488	8-23	S/Scr. Houston Compressed Steel 2-8-55
631		P-13	Baldwin	60513	8-28	Scr. Houston 1-4-54
632		P-13	Baldwin	60514	8-28	S/Scr. Commercial Metals, Houston 2-11-55
633		P-13	Baldwin	60564	8-28	S/Scr. Houston Compressed Steel 10-7-54
650	2455	P-14	American	53335	7-23-37	S/Scr. Houston Compressed Steel 3-25-54
651	2456	P-14	American	53336	8-7-37	S/Scr. Houston Compressed Steel 3-25-54
652	2457	P-14	American	53337	8-18-37	Scr. Houston 12-2-53

NOTES ABOUT THE ROSTER

This roster was compiled using data from a number of sources. First and foremost source was Southern Pacific's "Descriptive Record of Locomotive" file cards for each of the Pacific Lines locomotives. This collection of cards is now preserved at the California State Railroad Museum in Sacramento. In addition, Southern Pacific published and regularly updated employee handbooks called "Revised Classification and Assignment of Locomotives." Several of these from private collections were made available for this roster compilation.

Other published sources consulted include Gerald M. Best's roster in The Railway and Locomotive Historical Society Bulletin No. 94 (March 1956), Signor's and Kirchner's "Southern Pacific of Mexico" (1987), and Diebert's and Strapac's "Southern Pacific Company Steam Locomotive Compendium" (1987).

In addition, several working railroaders from the steam era kept meticulous notes. Two of these archivists, Jim Boynton and Bob McNeel, made their records available to me for this roster.

Every effort has been made to achieve accuracy in this roster. Numbers and dates were cross-checked in as many different sources as possible. Where data conflicted, information from Southern Pacific's file cards and handbooks superseded the other sources. The author solicits verifiable additional information or corrections for the roster.

Key to abbreviations used: Scr. = scrapped. S/Scr. = sold for scrap. Vac. = vacated. Re# = renumbered. Blt. = built. S.P.deMex. = Sud Pacifico de Mexico. T&NO = Texas & New Orleans. NWP = Northwestern Pacific. EP&SW = El Paso & Southwestern. Brooklyn is the name of Southern Pacific's shops in Portland, Oregon.

For most of the locomotives, the In-Service Date generally corresponds to the date built. Vacated Date shows when the locomotive was officially removed from the roster while Scrapped Date indicates when the locomotive was actually cut up.

Class P-10, Baldwin, 1924.   *Kenneth Roeh collection*

Index

Class P-12, American, 1917.   *Alco Historic Photos*